easy
British

easy British

100 fuss-free recipes for everyday cooking

M&S

Marks and Spencer plc
PO Box 3339
Chester CH99 9QS

shop online

www.marksandspencer.com

ISBN: 978-1-84960-980-7

Printed in China

Introduction by Linda Doeser
New recipes by Rachel Carter
Cover and additional photography by Mike Cooper
Cover and additional food styling by Lincoln Jefferson

The views expressed in this book are those of the author but they are general views only and readers are urged to consult a relevant and qualified specialist for individual advice in particular situations. Marks and Spencer plc and Exclusive Editions Limited hereby exclude all liability to the extent permitted by law for any errors or omissions in this book and for any loss, damage or expense (whether direct or indirect) suffered by a third party relying on any information contained in this book.

Notes for the Reader
This book uses both metric and imperial measurements. Follow the same units of measurement throughout; do not mix metric and imperial. All spoon measurements are level: teaspoons are assumed to be 5 ml, and tablespoons are assumed to be 15 ml. Unless otherwise stated, milk is assumed to be full fat, eggs and individual vegetables are medium, and pepper is freshly ground black pepper.

The times given are an approximate guide only. Preparation times differ according to the techniques used by different people and the cooking times may also vary from those given. Optional ingredients, variations or serving suggestions have not been included in the calculations.

Recipes using raw or very lightly cooked eggs should be avoided by infants, the elderly, pregnant women, convalescents and anyone suffering from an illness. Pregnant and breastfeeding women are advised to avoid eating peanuts and peanut products. Sufferers from nut allergies should be aware that some of the ready-made ingredients used in the recipes in this book may contain nuts. Always check the packaging before use.

For front cover recipe, please see page 114

Contents

Introduction

Given the superb quality of British produce, whether Scottish beef, Welsh lamb, Irish salmon or English cheese, it is heartening to see the renaissance of British cooking that has taken place over the last decade. Even in the past, when the mere idea of there being a British cuisine was – most unjustly – disparaged, some traditional dishes, ranging from the classic English breakfast and Sunday roast beef to traditional puddings and teatime cakes, were highly valued by international travellers and gourmets.

Regional dishes are the keystone of traditional British cooking. Apart from specialities from the nations that comprise Great Britain – Scotch Broth, Welsh Rarebit and Irish Stew, for example – there are many, diverse dishes that are characteristic of the history, geography and climate of the different regions, cities and institutions. The hard-pressed cotton mill and colliery workers of north-west England were the creators of the succulent lamb and potato stew known as Lancashire Hotpot, designed to ward off the chill of the bitter winter winds blowing across the Irish Sea. Cornish Pasties were all-in-one snacks for the tin miners whose dirty hands could hold the little pastry 'handles' without contaminating the contents, while Eton Mess,

a luxurious combination of strawberries, cream, meringue and liqueur, is still served at the annual prize-giving picnic at this school.

As well as producing top-quality meat, Britain has a long history of growing a huge variety of fruit and vegetables and this has given rise to an equally diverse range of delicious savoury and sweet dishes, desserts, cakes and preserves. An extensive range of cereal crops has resulted in a magnificent repertoire of cakes, biscuits, pies, tarts and breads. The relatively high rainfall in most of Britain produces lush grass that is ideal for raising dairy cattle, while the long coastline and numerous rivers and lakes offer scope for all manner of fresh and smoked fish and seafood.

As a rule, the British style of cooking is simple, to allow the flavours of these fine ingredients to speak for themselves, and the easy-to-follow recipes in this book make preparing these traditional favourites even more straightforward. Rich, lavish sauces are rare in traditional recipes, although simpler sauces, often variations of basic white sauce, feature in dishes as varied as Cauliflower Cheese and Fisherman's Pie. Above all, British cooking is home cooking – not dishes designed to impress with their stylish elegance, but tasty food to delight, nourish and comfort.

Top Tips for Success

• Life is very busy nowadays, and just because these are traditional recipes, it doesn't mean you have to revert to a 19th-century lifestyle. Make use of good-quality convenience ingredients, such as stock powder or ready-made stock from the chiller cabinet and chilled or frozen pastry dough.

• Similarly, use the microwave oven to save time. Melt chocolate by breaking it into pieces and heating on medium. Stir and check at 10-second intervals until almost completely melted, then stir in the last few tiny pieces. Soften butter by warming on high for 20 seconds. Toast nuts on high for 5 minutes.

• Whenever possible, buy seasonal produce, preferably locally sourced. Fresh fruit and vegetables that have not been subjected to lengthy transportation and storage will retain their texture, flavour and nutrients and be more economical.

• Ideally, use fish and seafood the day it is purchased; otherwise store in the refrigerator and use the following day.

• When using eggs, remember to remove them from the refrigerator about 30 minutes before they are needed to allow them to come to room temperature. They will foam better when whisked and omelettes will puff up appetizingly.

• Nowadays, good-quality sausages do not need to be pricked before cooking. They did in the past because they contained a lot of fat and water.

• Allow meat to rest, preferably on a rack, after cooking so that the juices and heat are evenly distributed. Allow about 3 minutes for chops and steak and 10–30 minutes for a roast.

• When making cakes, biscuits and breads, it is especially important to measure the ingredients accurately, as small variations in the proportions of ingredients can cause disaster. Use reliable scales, a measuring jug and proper measuring spoons.

• When making pies and crumbles, put the dish on a baking sheet before putting it in the oven. If there are any spills from the filling bubbling over, you won't have to clean the whole oven.

• When baking a cake, put a small ovenproof dish of water in the oven to prevent it from drying out or scorching.

• When storing home-made biscuits, put a spoonful of sugar in the same airtight container to help keep them crisp.

• Finally, instead of serving wine with dinner, why not try some traditional British ale or cider for a change?

1

The Big Breakfast

diy muesli

SERVES 4

50 g/1¾ oz rolled oats

**50 g/1¾ oz barley or
rye flakes**

**2 shredded wheat biscuits,
crushed**

**25 g/1 oz Brazil nuts,
roughly chopped**

25 g/1 oz hazelnuts

25 g/1 oz sunflower seeds

**50 g/1¾ oz ready-to-eat
dried apricots, chopped**

**2 red eating apples, cored
and roughly chopped,
to serve**

**150 ml/5 fl oz skimmed or
semi-skimmed milk,
to serve**

1 Mix together all the muesli ingredients in a large bowl.

2 When ready to serve, divide the muesli between the serving dishes.

3 Serve with the apples and milk.

TIP: You can vary the nuts, seeds and dried fruit to make a change, and add different fresh fruits as a topping. The muesli will keep for a few weeks in an airtight container, so double or quadruple quantities if required.

porridge

SERVES 1

300 ml/10 fl oz water

40 g/1½ oz coarse oats

salt

**muscovado sugar, honey
or golden syrup, to serve
(optional)**

1 Heat the water in a saucepan until boiling and pour in
the oats, stirring continuously.

2 Return to the boil and continue to stir for 2–3 minutes
(or according to the packet instructions).

3 Add salt to taste and serve immediately in a bowl,
stirring through muscovado sugar, honey or golden syrup,
if desired.

full english breakfast

SERVES 1

**2 good-quality
pork sausages**

**2–3 smoked back
bacon rashers**

**1 slice 2-day-old wholemeal
bread**

1 large tomato, halved

**vegetable oil, plus extra
for drizzling**

2–3 button mushrooms

1 egg

salt and pepper

1 Preheat the grill to high. Place the sausages under the hot grill and grill for about 15–20 minutes, turning frequently, until well browned. Keep warm.

2 Place the bacon rashers in a dry frying pan and fry for 2–4 minutes on each side. Remove from the frying pan, leaving all the excess bacon fat in the pan, and keep the bacon warm.

3 Heat the frying pan over a medium heat and place the bread in the fat. Cook for 1–2 minutes on one side, then turn over and repeat. Keep warm.

4 Place the tomato halves under the hot grill with the sausages. Drizzle with a little oil, season with salt and pepper to taste and grill for 3–4 minutes.

5 Add a little oil to a clean frying pan and fry the mushrooms. Remove from the pan and keep warm. Add the egg to the pan and fry, basting occasionally, for 1 minute, or until cooked to your liking.

6 Transfer the sausages, bacon, fried bread, tomatoes, mushrooms and egg to a plate and serve immediately.

eggs — the basics

SERVES 1

scrambling

2 eggs per person

15 g/½ oz butter

salt and pepper

frying

1–2 eggs per person

**1 tablespoon of oil or
15 g/½ oz butter**

poaching

1–2 eggs per person

1 Scrambling: Beat the eggs gently in a bowl with a little salt and pepper. Melt the butter in a saucepan over a low heat, pour in the beaten eggs and stir gently using a wooden spoon. As the egg starts to set, stir until it all looks creamy. Remove from the heat and stir until it does not look wet any more. Serve quickly to avoid them becoming rubbery.

2 Frying: The best way to fry an egg is in the same frying pan in which you have just fried some bacon. Otherwise, heat the oil or butter in a small frying pan over a medium heat. Break the egg into the frying pan (or break the egg into a cup first). Fry for a few seconds until the white sets, then baste with the fat to make sure the white is completely set and the yolk is still soft in the centre. Remove from the pan using a slotted spatula and serve immediately.

3 Poaching: Use a small shallow pan and really fresh eggs. Heat enough water to cover the eggs and break 1 egg into a cup. When the water is simmering gently, carefully pour in the egg and allow the white to coagulate around the yolk. Add another egg. Poach for 2–3 minutes for a soft yolk or for 4–5 minutes for a firmer egg. Remove from the pan using a slotted spoon, drain and serve immediately.

bacon butties with home-made tomato sauce

SERVES 2

tomato sauce (makes about 250 ml/9 fl oz)

2 tbsp olive oil

1 red onion, chopped

2 garlic cloves, chopped

250 g/9 oz plum tomatoes, chopped

250 g/9 oz canned chopped tomatoes

½ tsp ground ginger

½ tsp chilli powder

40 g/1½ oz dark brown sugar

100 ml/3½ fl oz red wine vinegar

salt and pepper

4 smoked bacon rashers

30 g/1 oz butter, softened

4 thick slices white or brown bread

pepper

1 Heat the oil in a large saucepan and add the onion, garlic and tomatoes. Add the ginger and chilli and season with salt and pepper to taste. Cook for 15 minutes, or until soft.

2 Pour the mixture into a food processor and blend well. Sieve thoroughly to remove all the seeds. Return the mixture to the pan and add the sugar and vinegar. Return to the boil and cook until it is the consistency of ketchup.

3 Bottle quickly in sterilized bottles or jars and store in a cool place or refrigerator until required.

4 Preheat the grill to high and grill the bacon, turning once, until it is crisp and golden brown. Spread the butter over the slices of bread.

5 Place two rashers on one slice of bread, season with pepper to taste and spoon or pour half the sauce over the bacon. Top with another slice of bread and repeat to make the second buttie. Serve immediately.

breakfast
omelette

SERVES 4

**4 pork or vegetarian
sausages**

small knob of butter

**2 tsp sunflower oil, plus
extra if necessary**

12 cherry tomatoes

6 eggs, beaten

salt and pepper

1 Preheat the grill to medium–high. Cook the sausages under the grill, turning frequently, until cooked through and well browned. Leave to cool slightly, then cut into bite-sized pieces.

2 Meanwhile, melt the butter with the oil in a medium-sized frying pan with a heatproof handle and cook the tomatoes, turning occasionally, for 2 minutes.

3 Add the sausage pieces to the frying pan, mixing evenly with the tomatoes. Add a little more oil if needed.

4 Season the eggs with salt and pepper to taste and pour over the sausages and tomatoes. Cook for 3 minutes, without stirring, then place the pan under the grill and cook the top for 3 minutes, or until set and lightly golden. Cut into wedges and serve immediately.

kedgeree

SERVES 4

**450 g/1 lb undyed smoked
haddock, skinned**

2 tbsp olive oil

1 onion, finely chopped

1 tsp mild curry paste

175 g/6 oz long-grain rice

55 g/2 oz butter

3 hard-boiled eggs

salt and pepper

**2 tbsp chopped fresh
parsley, to garnish**

1 Place the fish in a large saucepan and cover with water.
Bring to the boil, reduce the heat to a simmer and poach
the fish for 8–10 minutes until the flesh flakes easily.

2 Remove the fish and keep warm, reserving the water.

3 Add the oil to the saucepan and gently fry the onion for
about 4 minutes until soft. Stir in the curry paste and add
the rice.

4 Measure 600 ml/1 pint of the reserved haddock water
and return to the saucepan. Bring to a simmer and cover.
Cook for 10–12 minutes, or until the rice is tender. Season to
taste with salt and pepper.

5 Flake the fish and add to the saucepan with the butter.
Stir gently over a low heat until the butter has melted.
Chop 2 of the hard-boiled eggs and add to the saucepan.

6 Turn the kedgeree into a serving dish, slice the remaining
egg and use to garnish. Scatter the parsley over and
serve immediately.

sausages with mushrooms, bacon & tomatoes

SERVES 2

4 good-quality herbed sausages

4 tbsp grated Cheddar cheese

4 unsmoked streaky bacon rashers

2 tomatoes, halved horizontally

15 g/½ oz butter

1 tbsp olive oil

125 g/4½ oz button mushrooms, sliced

4 slices bread, crusts removed and buttered on both sides

salt and pepper

2 tbsp chopped fresh parsley, to garnish

1 Preheat the oven to 180°C/350°F/Gas Mark 4. Prick the sausages lightly, place in a roasting tin and roast for 10 minutes, or until just cooked. Remove and leave to cool. Make a slit in the sausages with a sharp knife and stuff each sausage with 1 tablespoon of the grated cheese. Wrap a bacon rasher around each sausage, tucking in the ends to secure. Return to the oven for a further 20 minutes, or until the bacon is cooked and the sausages are golden brown.

2 Meanwhile, place the tomatoes, cut-side up, on a baking tray and season to taste with salt and pepper. Roast for 15–20 minutes. Melt the butter with the oil in a medium-sized frying pan over a low heat, then add the mushrooms, stirring well to coat. Cover and cook for 5 minutes, or until the mushrooms are soft. Keep warm.

3 Heat a non-stick frying pan over a medium heat and cook the buttered bread in batches until golden brown on both sides. Keep warm. To serve, divide the fried bread between 2 plates and top with the mushrooms. Add the sausages and tomatoes and sprinkle with parsley.

eggs benedict with quick hollandaise sauce

SERVES 4

1 tbsp white wine vinegar

4 eggs

4 English muffins

4 slices good-quality ham

quick hollandaise sauce

3 egg yolks

200 g/7 oz butter

1 tbsp lemon juice

pepper

1 To make the hollandaise sauce, place the egg yolks in a blender or food processor. Melt the butter in a small saucepan until bubbling. With the motor running, gradually add the hot butter to the blender in a steady stream until the sauce is thick and creamy. Add the lemon juice, and a little warm water if the sauce is too thick, then season to taste with pepper. Remove from the blender or food processor and keep warm.

2 To poach the eggs, fill a frying pan three-quarters full with water and bring to a boil over a low heat. Reduce the heat to a simmer and add the vinegar. When the water is barely simmering, carefully break the eggs into the frying pan. Poach the eggs for 3 minutes, or until the whites are just set but the yolks are still soft.

3 Split the muffins and toast them on both sides. To serve, top each muffin with a slice of ham, a poached egg and a generous spoonful of hollandaise sauce.

kippers

SERVES 1

1 kipper

knob of butter

pepper

**slices of brown bread,
buttered, and lemon
wedges, to serve**

1 Place the kipper in a frying pan and cover with water.

2 Bring to the boil, then reduce the heat, cover and simmer gently for about 5 minutes.

3 Drain, pat dry with kitchen paper and place on a warm plate with a knob of butter on top. Season to taste with pepper.

4 Serve immediately with the buttered brown bread and a squeeze of lemon juice.

laverbread

SERVES 4

**4 tbsp prepared laver (laver
is an edible seaweed
that is greatly prized
in Wales)**

2 tbsp fine oatmeal

to serve

8 bacon rashers

4 tomatoes, halved

drizzle of oil

slices of hot, buttered toast

salt and pepper

1 Mix the laver with enough oatmeal to make it firm
enough to shape into 4 small round cakes.

2 Place the bacon rashers in a dry frying pan and fry
for 2–4 minutes on each side. Remove from the frying
pan, leaving all the bacon fat in the pan, and keep the
bacon warm.

3 Fry the laverbread in the hot bacon fat for 4–5 minutes
until nicely browned on one side. Turn over and repeat
until cooked through.

4 Preheat the grill to high. Drizzle the tomato halves with a
little oil, season with salt and pepper to taste and grill
for 3–4 minutes.

5 Serve the laver bread immediately with the fried bacon,
grilled tomatoes and toast.

devilled kidneys

SERVES 2

6 lambs' kidneys

3 tbsp flour

1 tsp cayenne pepper

1 tsp English mustard powder

25 g/1 oz butter

1 onion, finely sliced

1 tbsp tomato purée

1 tbsp Worcestershire sauce

350 ml/12fl oz chicken stock

salt and pepper

toasted wholemeal bread, to serve

1 First prepare the kidneys by removing and discarding any membrane on the outside. Then run them under cold water and pat dry with kitchen paper. Cut each one in half and snip out the white cores with kitchen scissors. Cut the kidneys into chunky pieces.

2 Mix the flour, cayenne and mustard powder together in a shallow bowl and season with salt and pepper. Toss the kidney pieces lightly in the mixture to coat.

3 Melt the butter in a frying pan and cook the onion for 6–8 minutes until softened and starting to brown. Add the kidneys and cook for 2–3 minutes, turning regularly.

4 Stir in the tomato purée, the Worcestershire sauce, the stock, season with salt and pepper and simmer over gentle heat for 15 minutes.

5 Serve immediately on chunky toasted wholemeal bread.

toasted cheese sandwich with egg

SERVES 1

2 slices crusty white or wholemeal bread

1 thick slice cooked ham

1 large tomato, thinly sliced

about 1 tbsp snipped fresh chives

small bunch of fresh flat-leaf parsley, stalks discarded

2 slices mild cheese, such as Wensleydale, Cheshire or mild Cheddar

olive oil

1 egg

small knob of soft butter (optional)

pepper

1 Preheat the grill to a medium–high heat. Prepare a small pan of simmering water or an egg poacher.

2 Toast the bread lightly on one side only under the grill. Top the toasted side of one of the slices of bread with the ham. Trim off any large areas of overhanging ham and place them on top. Overlap the tomatoes on the ham and sprinkle with the snipped chives and parsley. Top with the cheese slices. Season with pepper (there will probably be enough salt in the ham) and drizzle with a little olive oil, then cover with the second slice of bread, toasted side down.

3 Toast the sandwich on both sides until crisp and golden. Meanwhile, break the egg into a cup. Swirl the simmering water and drop the egg into the middle of the swirl, then poach it for about 3 minutes, until the white is set and the yolk is still soft. (Cook the egg for a shorter or longer time, to taste.) Alternatively, cook the egg in a poaching pan with cups. Use a slotted spoon to lift the egg from the pan, draining it thoroughly.

4 Serve the sandwich on a warmed plate, topped with the poached egg. Sprinkle with pepper and, if liked, add a small knob of butter so that it melts over the egg. Serve immediately.

potato cakes

SERVES 4

**550 g/1 lb 4 oz floury
potatoes, such as King
Edward, Maris Piper or
Desirée, cut into chunks**

**25 g/1 oz butter, plus extra
to serve**

1 egg (optional)

115 g/4 oz plain flour

oil, for greasing

salt and pepper

1 Bring a large saucepan of lightly salted water to the boil,
add the potatoes and cook for 15–20 minutes. Drain well
and mash with a potato masher until smooth. Season with
salt and pepper and add the butter. Mix in the egg, if using.

2 Turn out the mixture into a large mixing bowl and add
enough of the flour to make a light dough. Work quickly,
as you do not want the potato to cool too much.

3 Place the dough on a lightly floured surface and roll
out carefully to a thickness of 5 mm/¼ inch. Using a
6-cm/2½-inch pastry cutter, cut the dough into rounds.

4 Grease a griddle or heavy-based frying pan with a
little oil and heat. Slip the cakes onto the griddle in
batches and cook for 4–5 minutes on each side until they
are golden brown.

5 Keep the cooked cakes warm until ready to serve, then
serve on warmed plates with lots of fresh butter.

chive scrambled eggs on toast

SERVES 2

4 eggs

100 ml/3½ fl oz single cream

2 tbsp snipped fresh chives, plus extra to garnish

25 g/1 oz butter

4 slices brioche loaf

salt and pepper

1 Break the eggs into a medium bowl and whisk gently with the cream. Season to taste with salt and pepper and add the snipped chives.

2 Melt the butter in a sauté pan and pour in the egg mixture. Leave to set slightly, then move the mixture towards the centre of the pan using a wooden spoon as the eggs begin to cook. Continue in this way until the eggs are cooked but still creamy.

3 Lightly toast the brioche slices in a toaster or under the grill and place on two warmed plates. Spoon over the scrambled eggs and serve immediately, garnished with chives.

omelette arnold bennett

SERVES 2

175 g/6 oz undyed smoked haddock, skinned

25 g/1 oz butter

4 eggs, beaten

1 tbsp olive oil

4 tbsp single cream

2 tbsp grated Cheddar or Parmesan cheese

pepper

1 Place the fish in a large saucepan and cover with water. Bring the water to the boil, then reduce the heat to a simmer and poach the fish for 8–10 minutes until it flakes easily. Remove from the heat and drain onto a plate. When cool enough to handle, flake the fish and remove any bones. Melt half the butter in a small saucepan and add the haddock, to warm.

2 Season the eggs with pepper. The haddock will make it salty enough. Melt the remaining butter with the oil in a 23-cm/9-inch frying pan over a medium heat. When the butter starts to froth, pour in the eggs and spread them around by tilting the frying pan. Use a spatula or fork to move the egg around until it is cooked underneath but still liquid on top.

3 Preheat the grill to high. Tip in the hot haddock and spread over the omelette. Pour over the cream and top with the cheese, then place the frying pan under the grill for 1 minute until the cheese is melted. Serve immediately on hot plates.

bubble & squeak

SERVES 4

**450 g/1 lb floury potatoes,
such as King Edward,
Maris Piper or Desirée,
cut into chunks**

55 g/2 oz butter

3 tbsp hot milk

450 g/1 lb green cabbage

4 tbsp olive oil

1 onion, thinly sliced

salt and pepper

1 Bring a large saucepan of lightly salted water to the boil, add the potatoes and cook for 15–20 minutes. Drain well and mash with a potato masher until smooth. Season with salt and pepper, add the butter and milk and stir well.

2 Cut the cabbage into quarters, remove the stalk and finely shred the leaves.

3 Heat half the oil in a large frying pan, add the onion and fry until soft. Add the cabbage to the pan and stir-fry for 2–3 minutes until soft. Season with salt and pepper, add the potato and mix together well.

4 Press the mixture firmly into the frying pan and leave to cook over a high heat for 4–5 minutes until the base is crispy. Place a plate over the pan and invert the pan so that the potato cake falls onto the plate. Add the remaining oil to the pan, reheat and slip the cake back into the pan with the uncooked side down.

5 Continue to cook for a further 5 minutes until the base is crispy. Turn out onto a warmed plate and cut into wedges for serving. Serve immediately.

mushrooms on toast

SERVES 4

**12 slices baguette,
each 1 cm/½ inch thick,
or 2 individual baguettes,
cut lengthways**

3 tbsp olive oil

2 garlic cloves, crushed

**225 g/8 oz chestnut
mushrooms, sliced**

**225 g/8 oz mixed wild
mushrooms**

2 tsp lemon juice

**2 tbsp chopped fresh
parsley**

salt and pepper

1 Toast the bread on both sides until golden and keep warm.

2 Meanwhile, heat the oil in a frying pan. Add the garlic and cook gently for a few seconds, then add the chestnut mushrooms. Cook, stirring constantly, over a high heat for 3 minutes. Add the wild mushrooms and cook for a further 2 minutes. Stir in the lemon juice.

3 Season to taste with salt and pepper and stir in the chopped parsley.

4 Spoon the mushroom mixture on to the warm toast and serve immediately.

welsh rarebit

SERVES 4

**4 thick slices white or
brown bread**

**225 g/8 oz mature Cheddar
cheese, grated**

25 g/1 oz butter

3 tbsp beer

½ tsp mustard powder

1 egg, beaten

salt and pepper

1 Toast the bread under a medium grill on one side only.

2 Put the cheese into a saucepan and add the butter and beer. Heat slowly over a low heat, stirring continuously. Add some salt and pepper and the mustard powder and stir well until the mixture is thick and creamy. Remove from the heat and leave to cool slightly before mixing in the egg.

3 Spread the rarebit generously over the untoasted side of the bread and place under a hot grill until golden and bubbling. Serve immediately.

baked eggs with cream, spinach & parmesan

SERVES 2

**2 tbsp butter, plus extra
for greasing**

125 g/4½ oz baby spinach

**½ tsp freshly grated
nutmeg**

4 small eggs

4 tbsp single cream

**2 tbsp freshly grated
Parmesan cheese**

salt and pepper

1 Preheat the oven to 160°C/325°F/Gas Mark 3. Lightly grease 2 individual ceramic gratin dishes, or similar.

2 Melt the butter in a large frying pan over low heat and add the spinach. Cook for 1 minute, stirring with a wooden spoon until the spinach starts to wilt. Season with a little nutmeg, then divide between the prepared dishes.

3 Gently break 2 eggs into each dish. Pour the cream over them and sprinkle with grated Parmesan, then season with salt and pepper. Bake in the preheated oven for 10 minutes, or until the whites of the eggs have set but the yolks remain runny. Serve at once.

pancakes with baked mushrooms

SERVES 6

150 g/5½ oz plain white flour

1½ tsp baking powder

pinch of salt

250 ml/9 fl oz milk

1 large egg

2 tbsp melted butter

sunflower oil, for greasing

topping

55 g/2 oz butter

2 tbsp chopped parsley

1 tbsp chopped chives

1 garlic clove, crushed

3 tbsp olive oil

12 field mushrooms

salt and pepper

1 Preheat the oven to 200°C/400°F/Gas Mark 6. To make the topping, beat the butter until softened, stir in the parsley and chives and season to taste with salt and pepper.

2 Mix the garlic and oil together. Place the mushrooms on a baking sheet in a single layer, brush with the garlic oil and sprinkle with salt and pepper to taste. Bake in the oven for about 15 minutes, turning once, until tender.

3 Meanwhile, sift the flour, baking powder and salt into a bowl. Add the milk, egg and butter and whisk to a smooth batter. Leave to stand for 5 minutes.

4 Lightly grease a griddle pan or frying pan and heat over a medium heat. Spoon tablespoons of batter onto the pan and cook until bubbles appear on the surface.

5 Turn over with a palette knife and cook the other side until golden brown. Repeat this process using the remaining batter, while keeping the cooked pancakes warm.

6 Place a mushroom on each pancake, top with a spoonful of herb butter and serve immediately.

eggy bread

SERVES 2

1 large egg

4 tbsp milk or single cream

2 thick slices, day-old white bread

30 g/1 oz butter

1 Break the egg into a shallow bowl and whisk well. Stir in the milk.

2 Dip the bread into the egg mixture and coat both sides well.

3 Heat half the butter in a frying pan over a medium heat and gently fry one piece of eggy bread for about 1 minute on each side, or until golden brown and crispy. Take care not to let it burn. Remove from the pan and keep warm. Melt the remaining butter and repeat with the other piece of bread. Serve immediately.

breakfast smoothie

SERVES 2

250 ml/9 fl oz orange juice

125 ml/4 fl oz natural yogurt

2 eggs

2 bananas, sliced and frozen

slices of fresh banana, to decorate

1 Pour the orange juice and yogurt into a food processor and process gently until combined.

2 Add the eggs and frozen bananas and process until smooth.

3 Pour the mixture into glasses and decorate with a slice of fresh banana.

classic orange marmalade

MAKES ABOUT 4.5 KG/10 LB

1.5 kg/3 lb 5 oz Seville oranges, scrubbed

juice from 2 large lemons

3.4 litres/6 pints water

2.7 kg/6 lb preserving sugar

1 Cut the oranges in half and squeeze out all the juice. Scoop out all the pips from the orange shells and tie them up in a small piece of muslin. Slice the peel into small chunks or strips and place in a preserving pan together with the orange and lemon juice and water. Add the bag of pips.

2 Simmer gently for 1½ hours, or until the peel is very soft and the liquid has reduced by half. Remove the bag of pips, carefully squeezing to remove any juice. Add the sugar and heat, stirring, until the sugar has completely dissolved.

3 Bring to the boil and boil rapidly for about 15 minutes, or until the setting point is reached. Test if it is set by using a sugar thermometer. When it reads 105°C/221°F it is at a good setting point. Alternatively, test by dropping a small spoonful of marmalade onto a cold saucer, refrigerate to cool, then push with a clean finger. If it forms a wrinkled skin, it is ready. If not, boil the marmalade for a further minute and repeat.

4 Leave to cool slightly, then pot into warmed sterilized jars and cover the tops with waxed discs. When completely cold, cover with cellophane or lids, label and store in a cool place.

VARIATION

For a mixed peel marmalade, slice the peel from the lemons and use this instead of the peel from two of the oranges. Use all the juice from the fruit.

2

Everyday Essentials

creamy tomato & basil soup

SERVES 6

25 g/1 oz butter

1 tbsp olive oil

1 onion, finely chopped

1 garlic clove, chopped

900 g/2 lb plum tomatoes, chopped

700 ml/1¼ pints vegetable stock

125 ml/4 fl oz dry white wine

2 tbsp sun-dried tomato paste

2 tbsp torn fresh basil leaves, plus extra whole leaves to garnish

150 ml/5 fl oz double cream

salt and pepper

1 Melt the butter with the oil in a large heavy-based saucepan. Add the onion and cook, stirring occasionally, for 5 minutes, or until softened. Add the garlic, tomatoes, stock, wine and sun-dried tomato paste, stir well and season to taste with salt and pepper. Partially cover the saucepan and simmer, stirring occasionally, for 20–25 minutes, or until the mixture is soft and pulpy.

2 Remove the saucepan from the heat and leave to cool slightly. Transfer to a food processor or blender, in batches if necessary, add the torn basil and process to a purée. Push the mixture through a sieve into the rinsed-out pan.

3 Stir the cream into the soup and reheat gently, but do not let it boil. Ladle the soup into warmed bowls, garnish with whole basil leaves and serve immediately.

split pea
& ham soup

SERVES 6–8

500 g/1 lb 2 oz split green peas

1 tbsp olive oil

1 large onion, finely chopped

1 large carrot, finely chopped

1 celery stick, finely chopped

1 litre/1¾ pints chicken or vegetable stock

1 litre/1¾ pints water

225 g/8 oz lean smoked ham, finely diced

¼ tsp dried thyme

¼ tsp dried marjoram

1 bay leaf

salt and pepper

1 Rinse the split peas under cold running water. Put in a saucepan and add enough water to cover generously. Bring to the boil and boil for 3 minutes, skimming off any foam that rises to the surface. Drain.

2 Heat the oil in a large saucepan over a medium heat. Add the onion and cook, stirring occasionally, for 3–4 minutes, until just softened.

3 Add the carrot and celery and continue cooking for 2 minutes. Add the drained split peas, pour over the stock and water, and stir to combine.

4 Bring just to the boil and stir the ham into the soup. Add the thyme, marjoram and bay leaf. Reduce the heat, cover and cook gently for 1–1½ hours, until the ingredients are very soft. Remove and discard the bay leaf.

5 Taste and adjust the seasoning, adding salt and pepper if needed. Ladle into warmed bowls and serve immediately.

scotch broth

SERVES 6–8

**700 g/1 lb 9 oz neck of
lamb**

1.7 litres/3 pints water

55 g/2 oz pearl barley

2 onions, chopped

**1 garlic clove,
finely chopped**

3 small turnips, diced

3 carrots, finely sliced

2 celery sticks, sliced

2 leeks, sliced

salt and pepper

**2 tbsp chopped fresh
parsley, to garnish**

1 Cut the meat into small pieces, removing as much fat as possible. Put into a large saucepan and cover with the water. Bring to the boil over a medium heat and skim off any foam that appears.

2 Add the pearl barley, reduce the heat and cook gently, covered, for 1 hour.

3 Add the vegetables and season with salt and pepper to taste. Continue to cook for a further hour. Remove from the heat and allow to cool slightly.

4 Remove the meat from the saucepan using a slotted spoon and strip the meat from the bones. Discard the bones and any fat or gristle. Place the meat back in the saucepan and leave to cool thoroughly, then refrigerate overnight.

5 Scrape the solidified fat off the surface of the soup. Reheat, season with salt and pepper to taste and ladle into bowls. Serve immediately, garnished with the parsley.

broccoli & stilton soup

SERVES 6

40 g/1½ oz butter

2 white onions, chopped

1 large potato, chopped

750 g/1 lb 10 oz broccoli, cut into small florets

1.5 litres/2¾ pints vegetable stock

150 g/5½ oz Stilton cheese, diced

pinch of ground mace

salt and pepper

croûtons, to serve

1 Melt the butter in a large saucepan. Add the onions and potato and stir well. Cover and cook over a low heat for 7 minutes. Add the broccoli and stir well, then re-cover the pan and cook for a further 5 minutes.

2 Increase the heat to medium, pour in the stock and bring to the boil. Reduce the heat and season to taste with salt and pepper, then re-cover and simmer for 15–20 minutes, until the vegetables are tender.

3 Remove the pan from the heat, strain into a bowl, reserving the vegetables, and leave to cool slightly. Put the vegetables into a food processor or blender, add a ladleful of the liquid and process to a smooth purée. With the motor running, gradually add the remaining liquid.

4 Return the soup to the rinsed-out pan and reheat gently, but do not let it boil. Remove from the heat, add the cheese and stir in until melted and thoroughly combined. Stir in the mace, taste and adjust the seasoning, adding salt and pepper if needed.

5 Ladle into warmed bowls, sprinkle with croûtons and serve immediately.

cock-a-leekie

SERVES 6–8

2 tbsp vegetable or olive oil

2 onions, roughly chopped

2 carrots, roughly chopped

**5 leeks, 2 roughly chopped,
3 thinly sliced**

**1 chicken, weighing
1.3 kg/3 lb**

2 bay leaves

6 prunes, sliced

salt and pepper

**fresh flat-leaf parsley
sprigs, to garnish**

1 Heat the oil in a large saucepan over a medium heat. Add the onions, carrots and the roughly chopped leeks. Sauté for 3–4 minutes until just golden brown.

2 Wipe the chicken inside and out and remove any excess skin and fat.

3 Place the chicken in the saucepan with the cooked vegetables and add the bay leaves. Pour in enough cold water to just cover and season with salt and pepper to taste. Bring to the boil, reduce the heat, then cover and simmer for 1–1½ hours. Skim off any foam that appears.

4 Remove the chicken from the stock, skin, then remove all the meat. Cut the meat into equal-sized pieces.

5 Drain the stock through a colander, discard the vegetables and bay leaves and return the stock to the rinsed-out saucepan. Allow the stock to cool and skim off any fat that appears.

6 Heat the stock to simmering point, add the thinly sliced leeks and prunes to the saucepan and heat for about 1 minute. Return the chicken to the pan and heat through. Ladle into bowls, garnish with parsley sprigs and serve immediately.

fish & chips

SERVES 2

**vegetable oil, for
deep-frying**

**3 large potatoes, such as
Cara or Desirée**

**175 g/6 oz self-raising
flour, plus extra
for dusting**

200 ml/7 fl oz cold lager

**2 thick cod or haddock
fillets, 175 g/6 oz each**

salt and pepper

tartare sauce, to serve

1 Heat the oil in a deep-fat fryer to 120°C/250°F, or in a heavy-based saucepan, checking the temperature with a thermometer. Preheat the oven to 150°C/300°F/Gas Mark 2.

2 Peel the potatoes and cut into even-sized chips. Fry for about 8–10 minutes, depending on size, until soft but not coloured. Remove from the oil, drain on kitchen paper and place in a warmed dish in the preheated oven. Increase the temperature of the oil to 180–190°C/350–375°F, or until a cube of bread browns in 30 seconds.

3 Make a thick batter by sifting the flour into a bowl with a little salt and whisking in most of the lager. Check the consistency of the batter before adding the remaining lager: it should be very thick, like double cream.

4 Season the fish with salt and pepper and dust lightly with flour. Dip one fillet into the batter and allow the batter to coat it thickly. Carefully place the fish in the hot oil, then repeat with the other fillet.

5 Cook for 8–10 minutes, depending on the thickness of the fish. Turn over the fillets halfway through the cooking time. Remove the fish from the fryer, drain and keep warm.

6 Make sure the oil temperature is still at 180°C/350°F and return the chips to the fryer. Cook for a further 2–3 minutes until golden brown and crispy. Drain and season with salt and pepper before serving with the battered fish and tartare sauce.

fisherman's pie

SERVES 6

900 g/2 lb white fish fillets, such as plaice, skinned

150 ml/5 fl oz dry white wine

1 tbsp chopped fresh parsley, tarragon or dill

100 g/3½ oz butter, plus extra for greasing

175 g/6 oz small mushrooms, sliced

175 g/6 oz cooked, peeled prawns

40 g/1½ oz plain flour

125 ml/4 fl oz double cream

900 g/2 lb floury potatoes, such as King Edward, Maris Piper or Desirée, cut into chunks

salt and pepper

1 Preheat the oven to 180°C/350°F/Gas Mark 4. Grease a 1.7-litre/3-pint baking dish. Fold the fish fillets in half and place in the dish. Season well with salt and pepper, pour over the wine and scatter over the herbs. Cover with foil and bake for 15 minutes until the fish starts to flake. Strain off the liquid and reserve for the sauce. Increase the oven temperature to 220°C/425°F/Gas Mark 7.

2 Heat 15 g/½ oz of the butter in a frying pan and sauté the mushrooms. Spoon the mushrooms over the fish and scatter over the prawns.

3 Add 55 g/2 oz of the butter to a saucepan, heat and stir in the flour. Cook for a few minutes without browning, remove from the heat, then add the reserved cooking liquid gradually, stirring well between each addition.

4 Return to the heat and gently bring to the boil, still stirring to ensure a smooth sauce. Add the cream and season to taste with salt and pepper. Pour over the fish in the dish and smooth over the surface.

5 Make the mashed potato by cooking the potatoes in boiling salted water for 15–20 minutes. Drain well and mash with a potato masher until smooth. Season to taste with salt and pepper and add the remaining butter.

6 Pile or pipe the potato onto the fish and sauce and bake in the oven for 10–15 minutes until golden brown.

home–made fish fingers

SERVES 4–5

280 g/10 oz thick cod fillets, skin and bones removed

flour, for dusting

1 tsp paprika

fresh breadcrumbs or fine cornmeal, for coating

1 egg, beaten

sunflower oil, for frying

salt and pepper

fresh or frozen peas, cooked, to serve

sweet potato wedges

450 g/1 lb sweet potatoes, scrubbed and cut into wedges

1 tbsp olive oil

1 To make the potato wedges, preheat the oven to 200°C/400°F/Gas Mark 6. Dry the sweet potato wedges on a clean tea towel. Place the oil in a roasting tin and heat for a few minutes in the oven. Arrange the potatoes in the tin and bake for 30–35 minutes, turning them halfway through, until tender and golden.

2 Meanwhile, cut the cod into strips about 2-cm/ ¾-inch wide. Put the flour onto a plate, add the paprika and season to taste. Put the breadcrumbs onto a second plate. Roll the cod strips in the seasoned flour until coated, shaking off any excess, then dip them in the beaten egg. Roll the cod strips in the breadcrumbs until evenly coated.

3 Heat enough oil to cover the base of a large, non-stick frying pan. Carefully arrange the fish fingers in the pan – you may have to cook them in batches – and fry them for 3–4 minutes on each side or until crisp and golden. Drain on kitchen paper before serving, if necessary.

4 Serve the fish fingers with the sweet potato wedges and peas.

arbroath smokie pots

SERVES 4

1 tbsp melted butter

350 g/12 oz Arbroath smokies or other smoked fish, skinned

2 hard-boiled eggs, chopped

25 g/1 oz butter

25 g/1 oz plain flour

300 ml/10 fl oz milk

55 g/2 oz Cheddar cheese, grated

pinch of cayenne pepper

1 tbsp freshly grated Parmesan cheese

salt and pepper

brown toast slices, to serve

1 Preheat the oven to 180°C/350°F/Gas Mark 4. Use the melted butter to grease 4 small soufflé dishes or ramekins.

2 Flake the fish onto a plate, mix with the chopped egg and season with a little pepper. Place the mixture into the prepared dishes.

3 Melt the butter in a saucepan over a medium heat and stir in the flour. Cook for 1 minute, stirring continuously. Remove from the heat and stir in the milk gradually until smooth. Return to a low heat and stir until the sauce comes to the boil and thickens. Reduce the heat and simmer gently, stirring constantly, until the sauce is creamy and smooth.

4 Add the grated cheese and stir until melted, then season with salt and pepper to taste and add the cayenne pepper. Pour the sauce over the fish and egg mixture and sprinkle over the grated Parmesan cheese.

5 Place the ramekins on a baking tray and cook in the preheated oven for 10–15 minutes until bubbling and golden. Serve at once with brown toast.

cauliflower cheese

SERVES 4

**1 cauliflower, trimmed and
cut into florets (675 g/
1 lb 8 oz prepared
weight)**

40 g/1½ oz butter

40 g/1½ oz plain flour

450 ml/16 fl oz milk

**115 g/4 oz Cheddar cheese,
finely grated**

whole nutmeg, for grating

**1 tbsp grated Parmesan
cheese**

salt and pepper

1 Cook the cauliflower in a saucepan of boiling salted water for 4–5 minutes. It should still be firm. Drain, place in a hot 1.4-litre/2½-pint gratin dish and keep warm.

2 Melt the butter in the rinsed-out saucepan over a medium heat and stir in the flour. Cook for 1 minute, stirring continuously. Remove from the heat and stir in the milk gradually until you have a smooth consistency. Return to a low heat and continue to stir while the sauce comes to the boil and thickens. Reduce the heat and simmer gently, stirring constantly, for about 3 minutes until the sauce is creamy and smooth.

3 Remove from the heat and stir in the Cheddar cheese and a good grating of the nutmeg. Taste and season well with salt and pepper.

4 Preheat the grill to high. Pour the hot sauce over the cauliflower, top with the Parmesan and place under the grill to brown. Serve immediately.

cornish pasties

SERVES 4

**250 g/9 oz chuck steak,
trimmed and cut into
1-cm/½-inch dice**

**175 g/6 oz swede, cut into
1-cm/½-inch dice**

**350 g/12 oz potatoes, cut
into 1-cm/½-inch dice**

1 onion, finely chopped

1 egg, beaten

butter, for greasing

salt and pepper

pastry

**450 g/1 lb plain flour, plus
extra for dusting**

pinch of salt

115 g/4 oz lard

115 g/4 oz butter

175 ml/6 fl oz cold water

1 To make the pastry, sift the flour and salt into a bowl and gently rub in the lard and butter until the mixture resembles breadcrumbs. Add the water, a spoonful at a time, and stir the mixture with a knife until it holds together. Turn out onto a lightly floured surface and gently press together until smooth. Wrap in clingfilm and leave to chill for 1 hour.

2 Meanwhile, to prepare the filling, mix the meat and vegetables together and season well with salt and pepper.

3 Divide the pastry into four even-sized pieces and roll one out until just larger than the size of a 20-cm/8-inch plate. Place the plate on top of the pastry and cut round it to give a neat edge. Repeat with the other pieces.

4 Arrange the meat and vegetable mixture across the pastry, making sure the filling goes almost to the edge.

5 Brush the edges of the pastry with water, then bring the edges up over the filling and press together to form a ridge. You can flute the edges of the pasties with your fingers or fold over the pastry to form a seal. Tuck in the ends. Leave to chill for 1 hour, then glaze with the egg.

6 Preheat the oven to 190°C/375°F/Gas Mark 5 and grease a baking tray. Place the pasties on the baking tray and cook in the centre of the oven for 50–60 minutes. The pasties should be crisp and golden in colour. If the pastry is getting too brown, cover with foil and reduce the oven temperature. Serve warm.

ploughman's lunch

SERVES 4

4 large eggs

225 g/8 oz British cheese, such as farmhouse Cheddar cheese, Stilton and/or Somerset brie

300 g/10½ oz ready-made pork pie

1 carrot

8 spring onions

16 baby vine tomatoes

4 slices of cured, sliced ham

4 tbsp chutney of your choice

85g/3 oz salad leaves

crusty bread, to serve

1 First, boil the eggs. Bring a small pan of water to the boil. Gently lower the eggs into the water using a long-handled spoon. Keep the water at a gentle simmer and cook for 6–8 minutes, or until cooked to your liking. Remove the eggs using a slotted spoon and drain quickly on kitchen paper. Leave to cool.

2 When the eggs are cool enough to handle, remove and discard the shells. Cut the eggs in half. Cut the cheese into wedges and the pork pie into quarters. Peel the carrot and cut into batons.

3 Arrange all the ingredients on individual serving plates. Serve immediately, accompanied by crusty bread.

colcannon

SERVES 4

**450 g/1 lb floury potatoes,
cut into chunks**

55 g/2 oz butter

150 ml/5 fl oz single cream

**½ small green or white
cabbage**

**6 spring onions, finely
chopped**

salt and pepper

1 Cook the potatoes in a large saucepan of boiling salted water for 15–20 minutes. Drain well and mash with a potato masher until smooth. Season to taste with salt and pepper, add the butter and cream and stir well. The potato should be very soft. Keep warm.

2 Cut the cabbage into quarters, remove the centre stalk and shred the leaves finely. Cook the cabbage in a large saucepan of boiling salted water for just 1–2 minutes, until it is soft. Drain thoroughly.

3 Mix the potato and cabbage together and stir in the spring onions. Season well with salt and pepper.

4 Serve in individual bowls.

pork & apple pies

MAKES 8

900 g/2 lb waxy potatoes,
sliced

2 tbsp butter

2 tbsp vegetable oil

450 g/1 lb lean boneless
pork, cubed

2 onions, sliced

4 garlic cloves, crushed

600 ml/1 pint stock

2 tbsp chopped fresh sage

2 eating apples, peeled,
cored and sliced

1 egg, beaten

1 tsp gelatine

salt and pepper

pastry

675 g/1 lb 8 oz plain flour,
plus extra for dusting

pinch of salt

4 tbsp butter

125 g/4½ oz lard

300 ml/10 fl oz water

1 To make the filling, cook the potatoes in a saucepan of boiling water for 10 minutes. Drain and set aside. Melt the butter with the oil in a flameproof casserole over a medium–high heat. Add the pork and cook until browned all over.

2 Add the onions and garlic and cook, stirring frequently, for 5 minutes. Stir in the stock and sage. Season to taste with salt and pepper. Reduce the heat, cover and simmer for 1½ hours. Drain the stock from the casserole and reserve. Leave the pork to cool.

3 To make the pastry, sift the flour and salt into a bowl. Make a well in the centre. Melt the butter and lard in a saucepan with the water, then bring to the boil. Pour into the well and gradually mix into the flour to form a dough. Turn out onto a lightly floured surface and knead until smooth. Reserve a quarter of the dough and use the remainder to line the base and sides of 8 x 11-cm/4-inch pie tins.

4 Preheat the oven to 180°C/350°F/Gas Mark 4. Layer the pork, potatoes and apples in the base of the tins. Roll out the reserved pastry to make lids. Dampen the edges and put the lids on top, sealing well. Brush with the beaten egg to glaze. Make a hole in the top of each pie. Bake in the preheated oven for 30–40 minutes, or until the pastry is golden brown and the filling is cooked through. Dissolve the gelatine in the reserved stock and pour into the holes in the lids as the pies cool. Serve well chilled.

pan haggerty

SERVES 4–5

450 g/1 lb firm potatoes, such as Desirée or waxy salad potatoes

4 tbsp olive oil

55 g/2 oz butter

225 g/8 oz onions, halved and thinly sliced

115 g/4 oz Cheddar cheese, grated

salt and pepper

1 Peel the potatoes if necessary (you don't need to peel small salad potatoes). Slice thinly using a mandolin or food processor. Rinse the slices quickly in cold water and dry thoroughly using a tea towel or kitchen paper.

2 Heat half the olive oil and half the butter in a 23-cm/ 9-inch frying pan. Remove the frying pan from the heat and arrange the sliced potato in the base of the pan. Build up layers of potato, onion and cheese, seasoning well with salt and pepper between each layer. Finish with a layer of potato and dot the remaining butter over the top.

3 Return to the heat and cook over a medium heat for 15–20 minutes. The base should become brown but not burn. Place a large plate over the pan and invert the potato onto the plate by tilting the pan. Add the remaining oil to the pan and slip the potato back in, cooking the other side for a further 15 minutes until the base is crusty.

4 Remove from the heat and serve immediately on warmed plates.

egg & bacon pie

SERVES 4–6

pastry

100 g/3½ oz salted butter

200 g/7 oz plain flour, plus extra for dusting

1–2 tbsp cold water

filling

15 g/½ oz butter

1 small onion, finely chopped

4 lean streaky bacon rashers, diced

55 g/2 oz Cheddar cheese, grated

2 eggs, beaten

300 ml/10 fl oz single cream

pepper

1 For the pastry, rub the butter into the flour with your fingertips until the mixture resembles fine breadcrumbs. Stir in just enough water to bind the mixture to a firm dough. Roll out on a lightly floured surface and use to line a 23-cm/ 9-inch loose-based round tart tin. Prick the base all over with a fork. Chill for at least 10 minutes.

2 Preheat the oven to 200°C/400°C/Gas Mark 6. Line the pastry case with baking paper and beans, place on a baking tray and bake for 10 minutes. Remove the paper and beans and bake for a further 10 minutes.

3 For the filling, melt the butter in a frying pan and cook the onion and bacon for about 5 minutes until the onion is softened and lightly browned. Spread the mixture in the pastry case and sprinkle with half the cheese. Beat together the eggs and cream and season with pepper. Pour into the pastry case and sprinkle with the remaining cheese.

4 Reduce the oven temperature to 190°C/375°F/Gas Mark 5. Bake the pie for 25–30 minutes, or until golden brown and just set. Cool for 10 minutes before turning out.

macaroni cheese

SERVES 4

600 ml/1 pint milk

1 onion

8 peppercorns

1 bay leaf

55 g/2 oz butter

40 g/1½ oz plain flour

½ tsp ground nutmeg

5 tbsp double cream

**100 g/3½ oz mature
Cheddar cheese, grated**

**100 g/3½ oz Stilton cheese,
crumbled**

350 g/12 oz dried macaroni

**100 g/3½ oz Gruyère or
Emmental cheese,
grated**

pepper

1 Put the milk, onion, peppercorns and bay leaf in a pan
and bring to the boil. Remove from the heat and let
stand for 15 minutes.

2 Melt the butter in a pan and stir in the flour until well
combined and smooth. Cook over a medium heat, stirring
constantly, for 1 minute. Remove from the heat. Strain the
milk to remove the solids and stir a little into the butter and
flour mixture until well incorporated. Return to the heat and
gradually add the remaining milk, stirring constantly, until
it has all been incorporated. Cook for a further 3 minutes,
or until the sauce is smooth and thickened, then add the
nutmeg, cream and pepper to taste. Add the Cheddar and
Stilton cheeses and stir until melted.

3 Meanwhile, bring a large pan of water to the boil.
Add the macaroni, then return to the boil and cook for
8–10 minutes, or until just tender. Drain well and add to the
cheese sauce. Stir well together.

4 Preheat the grill to high. Spoon the macaroni mixture
into an ovenproof serving dish, then scatter over the
Gruyère cheese and cook under the grill until bubbling and
brown. Serve immediately.

pease pudding

SERVES 4-6

**350 g/12 oz dried split
green peas**

**1 carrot, finely diced
(optional)**

**1 celery stick,
finely diced (optional)**

**1 onion, finely chopped
(optional)**

**2 tsp vegetable stock
powder**

55 g/2 oz butter

**1 tbsp chopped fresh
mixed herbs**

1 egg, beaten

butter for greasing

salt and pepper

**boiled ham or gammon,
to serve**

1 Wash the peas well. Some dried varieties require soaking, if so, follow the directions provided on the pack.

2 Drain the peas, place in a saucepan and cover with fresh water. Place the saucepan over a medium heat and bring to the boil. Add the vegetables, if using, and the stock powder. If you have any meat bones, you could add these. Cook gently for 30–45 minutes until the peas are tender.

3 Remove from the heat and drain off the liquid (this can be retained to make soup) and remove any bones.

4 Purée the pea mixture using a mouli sieve or a food processor. Season well with salt and pepper and beat in the butter, herbs and the egg.

5 Spoon the mixture into a greased 600-ml/1-pint pudding basin, cover with greaseproof paper and foil. Steam the pudding in a covered pan half-filled with boiling water, for 1 hour, topping up with boiling water if needed. Turn out the pudding and serve with boiled ham or gammon.

scotch eggs

SERVES 4

4 large hard-boiled eggs

**300 g/10½ oz good-quality
sausage meat**

**1 tbsp plain flour, plus a
little more for shaping**

1 egg, beaten

**100 g/3½ oz fresh
breadcrumbs**

**vegetable oil, for
deep-frying**

salt and pepper

mixed green salad, to serve

1 Cool the eggs under cold running water. Peel carefully and wipe to make sure there are no pieces of shell attached to the eggs.

2 Divide the sausage meat into 4 equal portions and flatten out into rounds on a floured surface – they should be large enough to enclose the eggs.

3 Mix the flour with the salt and pepper to taste and put on a plate.

4 Put the beaten egg in a small bowl and the fresh breadcrumbs into a larger container.

5 Drop the eggs, one at a time, into the flour and then work the sausage meat around each egg until they are a good shape and have a smooth appearance. Brush with beaten egg and then toss in the breadcrumbs until evenly coated.

6 Heat the oil in a deep fat fryer to 150°C/300°F or in a heavy-based saucepan, checking the temperature with a thermometer. Fry the eggs for 6–8 minutes until they are golden brown. Remove them from the pan and drain well on kitchen paper. If using a saucepan, only cook two of the Scotch eggs at a time to be safe.

7 Cool completely, slice the Scotch eggs in half and serve immediately with a green salad.

cottage pie

SERVES 4

2 tbsp olive oil

1 large onion, finely chopped

2 small garlic cloves, finely chopped

1 carrot, diced

8 mushrooms, finely chopped

1 tsp dried oregano

280 g/10 oz fresh lean beef mince

300 ml/10 fl oz vegetable stock

150 ml/5 fl oz chopped tomatoes

2 tbsp tomato purée

4 potatoes, diced

2 heaped tbsp butter

4–6 tbsp milk

50 g/1¾ oz Cheddar cheese, grated

salt and pepper

1 Preheat the oven to 180°C/350°F/Gas Mark 4. Heat the oil in a heavy-based saucepan and cook the onion and garlic, stirring occasionally, for 8 minutes, or until softened. Add the carrot, mushrooms and oregano and cook for 5 minutes. Add the mince and cook, stirring, until browned.

2 Add the stock, tomatoes and tomato purée and bring to the boil, then reduce the heat and simmer, partially covered, for 10–15 minutes, or until the sauce has thickened and reduced. Season to taste with salt and pepper.

3 Meanwhile, cook the potatoes in a saucepan of boiling water for 10 minutes, or until tender. Drain, return to the saucepan and mash with the butter and milk.

4 Put the mince in an ovenproof casserole dish or 4 individual dishes. Spoon over the mash and top with the cheese. Bake in the preheated oven for 20 minutes, or until golden.

chicken liver pâté

SERVES 4–6

200 g/7 oz butter

225 g/8 oz trimmed chicken livers, thawed if frozen

2 tbsp Marsala or brandy

1½ tsp chopped fresh sage

1 garlic clove, roughly chopped

150 ml/5 fl oz double cream

salt and pepper

fresh bay leaves or sage leaves, to garnish

crackers, to serve

1 Melt 40 g/1½ oz of the butter in a large, heavy-based frying pan. Add the chicken livers and cook over a medium heat for about 4 minutes on each side. They should be browned on the outside but still pink in the middle. Transfer to a food processor and process until finely chopped.

2 Stir the Marsala or brandy into the pan, scraping up any sediment with a wooden spoon, then add to the food processor with the chopped sage, garlic and 100 g/3½ oz of the remaining butter. Process until smooth. Add the cream, season with salt and pepper and process until thoroughly combined and smooth. Spoon the pâté into a dish or individual ramekins, smooth the surface and leave to cool completely.

3 Melt the remaining butter, then spoon it over the surface of the pâté. Decorate with herb leaves, cool, then chill in the refrigerator. Serve with crackers.

ham, egg & chips

SERVES 4

**vegetable oil, for frying
and brushing**

**6 large potatoes, such as
Desirée or Maris Piper,
cut into even-sized chips**

**4 x 175 g/6 oz gammon
steaks**

4 eggs

1 Heat enough oil for deep-frying in a large saucepan or deep-fryer to 120°C/250°F, checking the temperature with a thermometer. Preheat the oven to 150°C/300°F/Gas Mark 2.

2 Fry the chips for about 8–10 minutes, depending on size, until soft but not coloured. Remove from the oil, drain on kitchen paper and place in a warmed dish in the preheated oven. Increase the temperature of the oil to 180–190°C/350–375°F, or until a cube of bread browns in 30 seconds.

3 Preheat the grill to high, brush the gammon steaks with a little oil and grill for 3–4 minutes on either side, turning occasionally until the fat is crisp. Set aside and keep warm.

4 Return the chips to the fryer at the increased temperature and cook for a further 2–3 minutes until they are golden brown and crisp. Drain and keep warm.

5 Put 2 tablespoons of oil into a frying pan and heat over a medium heat. Break two eggs into the pan and cook for a few seconds until the white is setting. Tip the pan and spoon the hot oil over the egg yolks so that they become firm but still soft. Remove the eggs from the pan using a wooden spatula and drain on kitchen paper. Keep warm and repeat with the other eggs.

6 Arrange the gammon steaks, egg and chips on warmed plates and serve immediately.

toad-in-the-hole

SERVES 4

115 g/4 oz plain flour

pinch of salt

1 egg, beaten

300 ml/10 fl oz milk

**450 g/1 lb good-quality
pork sausages**

**1 tbsp vegetable oil,
plus extra for greasing**

1 Make the batter by sifting the flour and salt into a mixing bowl. Make a well in the centre and add the beaten egg and half the milk. Carefully stir the liquid into the flour until the mixture is smooth. Gradually beat in the remaining milk. Leave to stand for 30 minutes.

2 Grease a 20 x 25-cm/8 x 10-inch ovenproof dish or roasting tin. Preheat the oven to 220°C/425°F/Gas Mark 7.

3 Prick the sausages and place them in the dish. Sprinkle over the oil and cook the sausages in the oven for 10 minutes until they are beginning to colour and the fat has started to run and is sizzling.

4 Remove from the oven and quickly pour the batter over the sausages. Return to the oven and cook for 35–45 minutes until the batter is well risen and golden brown. Serve immediately.

sausages & mash with onion gravy

SERVES 4

1 tbsp olive oil

8 good-quality sausages

onion gravy

3 onions, cut in half and thinly sliced

70 g/2½ oz butter

125 ml/4 fl oz Marsala or port

125 ml/4 fl oz vegetable stock

mashed potato

900 g/2 lb floury potatoes, such as King Edward, Maris Piper or Desirée, cut into chunks

55 g/2 oz butter

3 tbsp hot milk

salt and pepper

2 tbsp chopped fresh parsley

salt and pepper

1 Prepare the onion gravy by placing the onions in a frying pan with the butter and frying over a low heat until soft, stirring continuously. Continue to cook for around 30 minutes, or until the onions are brown and have started to caramelize. Pour in the Marsala and stock and continue to bubble away until the onion gravy is really thick. Season to taste with salt and pepper.

2 Meanwhile, cook the sausages. Place a frying pan over a low heat with the oil and add the sausages. Cover the pan and cook for 25–30 minutes, turning the sausages from time to time, until browned all over.

3 To make the mashed potato, cook the potatoes in a large saucepan of lightly salted boiling water for 15–20 minutes. Drain well and mash with a potato masher until smooth. Season with salt and pepper to taste, add the butter, milk and parsley and stir well.

4 Serve the sausages immediately with the mashed potato and the onion gravy spooned over the top.

VARIATION
For a tasty alternative, serve with Colcannon (see page 84) instead of plain mashed potato.

Weekend Specials

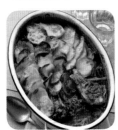

roast beef

SERVES 8

2.7 kg/6 lb prime rib of beef

2 tsp dry English mustard

3 tbsp plain flour

300 ml/10 fl oz red wine

300 ml/10 fl oz beef stock

2 tsp Worcestershire sauce (optional)

salt and pepper

Yorkshire puddings, to serve

1 Preheat the oven to 230°C/450°F/Gas Mark 8. Season the meat with salt and pepper to taste and rub in the mustard and 1 tablespoon of the flour.

2 Place the meat in a roasting tin and cook for 15 minutes. Reduce the heat to 190°C/375°F/Gas Mark 5 and cook for 15 minutes per 450 g/1 lb, plus 15 minutes (1 hour 45 minutes for this joint) for rare beef, or 20 minutes per 450 g/1 lb, plus 20 minutes (2 hours 20 minutes) for medium beef. Baste the meat from time to time to keep it moist and if the tin becomes too dry, add a little red wine or stock.

3 Remove the meat from the oven and place on a hot serving plate, cover with foil and leave in a warm place for 10–15 minutes.

4 To make the gravy, pour off most of the fat from the tin, leaving behind the meat juices and the sediment. Place the tin on the top of the hob over a medium heat and scrape all the sediment from the base of the tin. Sprinkle in the remaining flour and quickly mix it into the juices with a small whisk. When you have a smooth paste, gradually add the wine and most of the stock, whisking all the time. Bring to the boil, then turn down the heat to a gentle simmer and cook for 2–3 minutes. Season with salt and pepper to taste and add the remaining stock, if needed, and a little Worcestershire sauce, if using.

5 Carve the meat into slices and serve immediately with the gravy and Yorkshire puddings.

beef wellington

2 tbsp olive oil or vegetable oil

1.5 kg/3 lb 5 oz beef fillet, cut from the middle of the fillet, trimmed of fat and sinew

55 g/2 oz butter

150 g/5½ oz mushrooms, chopped

2 garlic cloves, crushed

150 g/5½ oz smooth liver pâté

few drops of truffle oil (optional)

1 tbsp fresh parsley, finely chopped

2 tsp English mustard

500 g/1 lb 2 oz ready-made puff pastry

1 egg, lightly beaten

salt and pepper

wilted greens and roasted root vegetables, including parsnips, to serve

1 Place a large frying pan over a high heat and add the olive oil. Rub salt and pepper into the beef, place it in the pan and sear very quickly all over. (This method gives a rare version. If you want it less rare, roast it at 200°C/400°F/Gas Mark 6, for 20 minutes at this stage.) Set aside to cool.

2 Heat the butter in a frying pan over a medium heat, add the mushrooms and fry for 5 minutes. Reduce the heat, add the garlic and fry for a further 5 minutes. Put the mushrooms and garlic in a bowl, add the pâté, truffle oil, if using, and parsley, and mash with a fork. Leave to cool.

3 Rub the mustard into the seared beef fillet. Roll out the pastry into a rectangle large enough to wrap the whole fillet with some to spare. Spread the mushroom paste in the middle of the pastry in a shape the size of the base of the beef and lay the beef on top. Brush the edges of the pastry with half of the beaten egg and fold it over, edges overlapping, and across the meat to completely enclose it.

4 Preheat the oven to 200°C/400°F/Gas Mark 6. Place the wrapped beef in a roasting tin with the join underneath and brush with the remaining beaten egg. Leave to chill in the refrigerator for 15 minutes, then transfer to the preheated oven and bake for 50 minutes. Check after 30 minutes – if the pastry looks golden brown, cover it with foil to prevent it burning.

5 Carve the beef into thick slices and serve on warmed plates with wilted greens and roasted root vegetables.

chicken, mushroom & tarragon pie

SERVES 4–6

filling

1 chicken, about 1.5 kg/ 3 lb 5 oz

2 fresh tarragon sprigs

1 Spanish onion, cut into wedges

300 ml/10 fl oz water

25 g/1 oz butter

175 g/6 oz chestnut mushrooms, sliced

2 tbsp plain flour

55 g/2 oz frozen or shelled fresh peas

1 tbsp chopped fresh tarragon

salt and pepper

pastry

225 g/8 oz plain flour, plus extra for dusting

pinch of salt

175 g/6 oz butter

4 tbsp iced water

1 egg, lightly beaten

1 Preheat the oven to 200°C/400°F/Gas Mark 6. Put the chicken, tarragon sprigs and onion into a casserole, add the water and season. Cover and bake for 1½ hours. Remove the chicken. Strain the juices into a measuring jug and chill. Discard the chicken skin, cut off the meat and dice. Skim off the fat from the cooking juices and make up to 300 ml/ 10 fl oz with water.

2 To make the pastry, sift the flour with the salt into a bowl and add the butter and water. Mix to a firm but slightly lumpy dough, adding more iced water if necessary. Roll out into a rectangle on a lightly floured surface, then fold the top third down and the bottom third up. Give the dough a quarter turn, roll out and fold again. Repeat once more, then wrap and chill for 30 minutes.

3 Melt the butter in a pan. Cook the mushrooms over a medium heat for 3 minutes. Stir in the flour for 1 minute, then gradually stir in the cooking juices. Bring to the boil, add the chicken, peas and tarragon and season to taste. Transfer to a large pie dish and cool.

4 Preheat the oven to 200°C/400°F/Gas Mark 6. Roll out the pastry slightly larger than the top of the dish. Cut a narrow strip of pastry, brush the rim of the dish with water and press the strip around the rim. Brush with water and lift the pastry on top. Trim and crimp the edges to seal. Make a slit in the centre and brush with beaten egg. Decorate the pie with the trimmings, then brush with beaten egg. Bake for 40 minutes, until golden. Serve immediately.

crown roast of lamb

SERVES 6

1.6 kg/3 lb 8 oz (18 bone) crown of lamb (ask your butcher to prepare)

2 tbsp olive oil

salt and pepper

stuffing

100 g/3½ oz wild and long grain rice

2 tbsp vegetable oil

1 onion, finely chopped

2 sticks celery, finely chopped

2 garlic cloves, crushed

25 g/1 oz shelled, unsalted pistachios

1 lemon, zest finely grated, juice of ½ lemon

2 tbsp finely chopped mint

2 tbsp finely chopped flat leaf parsley

100 g/3½ oz raisins

1 Calculate the cooking time of the lamb by allowing 25 minutes per 450 g/1lb plus 25 minutes for medium, or 30 minutes per 450 g/1lb plus 30 minutes for well done. Place the crown in a deep roasting tin, brush the outside with oil and season with salt and pepper. Preheat the oven to 180°C/350°F/Gas Mark 4.

2 To make the stuffing, cook the rice until just al dente. Drain and cool. Heat the oil in a frying pan and sauté the onion and celery for 4–5 minutes. Add the garlic and cook for a further 1 minute until softened but not browned. Stir into the cooled rice, together with the pistachios, lemon zest and juice, herbs and raisins.

3 Fill the centre of the crown with the stuffing, cover the ends of the bones with foil to prevent burning, then cover the whole joint with foil. Roast for the calculated time, removing the foil for the last 10–15 minutes.

4 At the end of the cooking time, remove from the oven, lift out of the tin, re-cover completely with foil and allow to rest for 20 minutes. Serve with the stuffing.

lancashire hotpot

SERVES 4–6

900 g/2 lb best end lamb chops

3 lambs' kidneys, cored and quartered

55 g/2 oz butter

900 g/2 lb floury potatoes, such as King Edward or Maris Piper, sliced

3 onions, halved and finely sliced

2 tsp fresh thyme leaves

1 tsp finely chopped fresh rosemary

600 ml/1 pint chicken stock

salt and pepper

1 Preheat the oven to 160°C/325°F/Gas Mark 3.

2 Trim the chops of any excess fat and place in a bowl. Add the kidneys to the bowl and season with salt and pepper to taste.

3 Grease a large, shallow ovenproof dish or deep roasting tin with half the butter and arrange a layer of potatoes in the bottom. Layer up the onions and meat, seasoning with salt and pepper to taste and sprinkling in the herbs between each layer. Finish with a neat layer of overlapping potatoes.

4 Pour in most of the stock so that it covers the meat. Melt the remaining butter and brush the top of the potato with it. Reserve any remaining butter. Cover with foil and cook in the preheated oven for 2 hours.

5 Uncover the hotpot and brush the potatoes again with the melted butter.

6 Return the hotpot to the oven and cook for a further 30 minutes, or until the potatoes are crisp and brown Serve the hotpot immediately.

roast chicken

SERVES 6

**1 chicken, weighing
2.25 kg/5 lb**

55 g/2 oz butter

**2 tbsp chopped fresh lemon
thyme**

1 lemon, quartered

125 ml/4 fl oz white wine

salt and pepper

**6 sprigs of fresh thyme,
to garnish**

1 Preheat the oven to 220°C/425°F/Gas Mark 7. Wipe the chicken well with kitchen paper, inside and out, and place in a roasting tin.

2 Place the butter in a bowl and soften with a fork, then mix in the lemon thyme and season well with salt and pepper. Butter the chicken all over with the herb butter, inside and out, and place the lemon pieces inside the body cavity. Pour the wine over the chicken.

3 Roast in the centre of the preheated oven for 20 minutes. Reduce the temperature to 190°C/375°F/Gas Mark 5 and continue to roast for a further 1¼ hours, basting frequently. Cover with foil if the skin begins to brown too much. If the tin dries out, add a little more wine or water.

4 Test that the chicken is cooked by piercing the thickest part of the leg with a sharp knife or skewer and making sure the juices run clear. Remove from the oven.

5 Remove the chicken from the roasting tin and place on a warmed serving plate, cover with foil and leave to rest for 10 minutes before carving.

6 Place the roasting tin on the hob over a low heat and bubble the pan juices gently until they have reduced and are thick and glossy. Season with salt and pepper.

7 Serve the chicken with the pan juices and scatter with the thyme sprigs.

irish stew

SERVES 4

4 tbsp plain flour

1.3 kg/3 lb middle neck of lamb, trimmed of visible fat

3 large onions, chopped

3 carrots, sliced

450 g/1 lb potatoes, cut into wedges

½ tsp dried thyme

850 ml/1½ pints hot beef stock

salt and pepper

2 tbsp chopped fresh parsley, to garnish

1 Preheat the oven to 160°C/325°F/Gas Mark 3. Spread the flour on a plate and season with salt and pepper to taste. Roll the pieces of lamb in the flour to coat, shaking off any excess, and arrange in the base of a casserole.

2 Layer the onions, carrots and potatoes on top of the lamb.

3 Sprinkle in the thyme and pour in the stock, then cover and cook in the preheated oven for 2½ hours. Serve immediately, garnished with the parsley.

glazed gammon cooked in cider

SERVES 8

4-kg/9-lb gammon

1 apple, cored and chopped

1 onion, chopped

300 ml/10 fl oz cider

6 black peppercorns

1 bouquet garni

1 bay leaf

about 50 cloves

4 tbsp demerara sugar

1 Put the gammon in a large saucepan and add enough cold water to cover. Bring to the boil and skim off any foam that rises to the surface. Reduce the heat and simmer for 30 minutes.

2 Drain the gammon and return to the saucepan. Add the apple, onion, cider, peppercorns, bouquet garni, bay leaf and a few of the cloves. Pour in enough fresh water to cover and bring back to the boil. Cover and simmer for 3 hours 20 minutes.

3 Preheat the oven to 200°C/400°F/Gas Mark 6. Take the saucepan off the heat and set aside to cool slightly. Remove the gammon from the cooking liquid and, while it is still warm, loosen the rind with a sharp knife, then peel it off and discard.

4 Score the fat into diamond shapes and stud with the remaining cloves. Place the gammon on a rack in a roasting tin and sprinkle with the sugar. Roast in the preheated oven, basting occasionally with the cooking liquid, for 20 minutes. Serve hot or cold.

poached salmon with hollandaise sauce

SERVES 8

melted butter, for greasing

1.8 kg/4 lb whole fresh salmon, gutted

1 lemon, sliced

sprigs of fresh parsley

125 ml/4 fl oz white wine or water

salt and pepper

sprigs of fresh parsley, to garnish

lemon wedges, to serve

hollandaise sauce

2 tbsp white wine vinegar

2 tbsp water

6 black peppercorns

3 egg yolks

250 g/9 oz unsalted butter

2 tsp lemon juice

salt and pepper

1 Preheat the oven to 150°C/300°F/Gas Mark 2. Line a large roasting tin with a double layer of foil and brush with butter. Trim off the fins then season the salmon with salt and pepper, inside and out. Lay on the foil and place the lemon slices and parsley in the body cavity. Pour over the wine and gather up the foil to make a fairly loose parcel.

2 Place the tin in the preheated oven and bake for 50–60 minutes. Test the salmon with the point of a knife: the flesh should flake when the fish is cooked. Remove from the oven and leave to stand for 15 minutes before removing from the foil to serve hot. To serve cold, leave for 1–2 hours until lukewarm, then carefully remove from the foil and peel away the skin from the top side, leaving the head and tail intact.

3 Meanwhile, to make the hollandaise sauce, put the vinegar and water into a small saucepan with the peppercorns, bring to the boil, then reduce the heat and simmer until it is reduced to 1 tablespoon, then strain. Mix the egg yolks in a blender or food processor and add the strained vinegar while the machine is running. Melt the butter in a small saucepan and heat until it almost turns brown. Again, while the blender is running, add three quarters of the butter, the lemon juice and the remaining butter and season well with salt and pepper.

4 Serve the salmon garnished with parsley, and with lemon wedges and hollandaise sauce on the side.

fish cakes

SERVES 4

450 g/1 lb floury potatoes, such as King Edward, Maris Piper or Desirée, cut into chunks

450 g/1 lb mixed fish fillets, such as cod and salmon, skinned

2 tbsp chopped fresh tarragon

grated rind of 1 lemon

2 tbsp double cream

1 tbsp plain flour

1 egg, beaten

115 g/4 oz breadcrumbs, made from day-old white bread or wholemeal bread

4 tbsp vegetable oil, for frying

salt and pepper

watercress salad and lemon wedges, to serve

1 Bring a large saucepan of lightly salted water to the boil, add the potatoes and cook for 15–20 minutes. Drain well and mash with a potato masher until smooth.

2 Place the fish in a frying pan and just cover with water. Bring to the boil over a medium heat, then reduce the heat, cover the pan and simmer gently for 5 minutes until cooked.

3 Remove the pan from the heat and drain the fish onto a plate. When cool enough to handle, flake the fish roughly into good-sized pieces, ensuring that there are no bones.

4 Mix the potato with the fish, tarragon, lemon rind and cream. Season well with salt and pepper and shape into four round cakes or eight smaller ones.

5 Dust the cakes with flour and dip them into the beaten egg, then coat thoroughly with the breadcrumbs. Place on a baking tray and leave to chill for at least 30 minutes.

6 Heat the oil in the pan, add the cakes and fry over a medium heat for 5 minutes on each side, turning them carefully with a palette knife or a fish slice.

7 Serve immediately with a watercress salad and lemon wedges.

seafood pie with stilton

SERVES 6

300 ml/10 fl oz vegetable stock

100 ml/3½ fl oz dry vermouth

3 tbsp cornflour, blended with 3 tbsp cold water

30 g/1 oz butter, cut into small pieces

6 tbsp crème fraîche

375 g/13 oz skinless cod fillet, cut into chunks

375 g/13 oz skinless salmon fillet, cut into chunks

225 g/8 oz raw king prawns, peeled, deveined

175 g/6 oz fine asparagus spears, tough ends snapped off, cut into 2.5-cm/1-inch pieces

115 g/4 oz Stilton cheese, crumbled

4 tbsp snipped fresh chives

500 g/1 lb 2oz ready-made puff pastry

plain flour, for dusting

pepper

1 Pour the stock and vermouth into a saucepan and bring to the boil. Whisk in the cornflour paste and simmer for 1 minute to make a thick sauce. Remove from heat and stir in the butter and crème fraîche, then cover the surface with baking paper. Leave to cool.

2 Preheat the oven to 220°C/425°F/Gas Mark 7. Stir the fish, prawns, asparagus, Stilton and chives into the sauce. Season to taste with pepper, then spoon into a 1.4-litre/2½-pint pie dish.

3 Roll out the pastry on a lightly floured surface to a thickness of about 3 mm/⅛ inch. Cut a long 2-cm/¾-inch strip and press around the rim of the pie dish, fixing it in place with a little water. Use the remaining pastry to cover the pie, cutting the trimmings into shapes to decorate and fixing into place with a little water. Make a small hole in the centre to allow steam to escape.

4 Bake in the preheated oven for 20 minutes, until the pastry is well risen and golden brown, then reduce the temperature to 180°C/350°F/Gas Mark 4 and bake for a further 35 minutes. Serve immediately.

trout with almonds

SERVES 2

2 fresh trout

55 g/2 oz salted butter

55 g/2 oz flaked almonds

2 tbsp chopped fresh parsley

3 tbsp fresh lemon juice

salt and pepper

selection of steamed vegetables, to serve

1 Season the fish with salt and pepper on both sides. Melt the butter in a large frying pan and fry the trout on each side for 6–8 minutes, until golden brown and cooked through.

2 Remove the fish to a heated serving dish and place in a warm oven. Add the flaked almonds to the frying pan, turning until they are golden brown. Add the parsley and the lemon juice, which will all combine into a lovely herby, lemony sauce.

3 Arrange the trout on a serving plate and spoon over the sauce. The fish is delicious with a selection of steamed vegetables such as baby carrots and sweetcorn, broccoli and some new potatoes.

perfect roast potatoes

SERVES 6

70 g/2½ oz goose or duck fat or 5 tbsp olive oil

1 kg/2 lb 4 oz even-sized potatoes

coarse sea salt

1 Preheat the oven to 230°C/450°F/Gas Mark 8. Put the fat in a large roasting tin, sprinkle generously with sea salt and place in the oven.

2 Meanwhile, cook the potatoes in a large saucepan of boiling water for 8–10 minutes until parboiled. Drain well and, if the potatoes are large, cut them in half. Return the potatoes to the empty saucepan and shake vigorously to roughen their outsides.

3 Arrange the potatoes in a single layer in the hot fat and roast for 45 minutes. If they look as if they are beginning to char around the edges, reduce the oven temperature to 200°C/400°F/Gas Mark 6. Turn the potatoes over and roast for a further 30 minutes until crisp. Serve immediately.

honeyed parsnips

SERVES 4

8 parsnips, quartered

4 tbsp vegetable oil

1 tbsp honey

1 Preheat the oven to 180°C/350°F/Gas Mark 4.

2 Bring a large saucepan of water to the boil. Reduce the heat, add the parsnips and cook for 5 minutes. Drain thoroughly.

3 Pour 2 tablespoons of the oil into a shallow ovenproof dish and add the parsnips. Mix the remaining oil with the honey and drizzle over the parsnips. Roast in the preheated oven for 45 minutes, until golden brown and tender. Remove from the oven and serve.

brussels sprouts with chestnuts

SERVES 4

350 g/12 oz Brussels sprouts

3 tbsp butter

100 g/3½ oz canned whole chestnuts

pinch of nutmeg

salt and pepper

50 g/1¾ oz flaked almonds, to garnish

1 Bring a large saucepan of water to the boil. Add the Brussels sprouts and cook for 5 minutes. Drain thoroughly.

2 Melt the butter in a large saucepan over a medium heat. Add the Brussels sprouts and cook, stirring, for 3 minutes.

3 Add the chestnuts and nutmeg to the pan. Season with salt and pepper and stir well. Cook for a further 2 minutes, stirring, then remove from the heat.

4 Transfer to a serving dish, scatter over the almonds and serve.

gooseberry fool

SERVES 6

700 g/1 lb 9 oz gooseberries

25 g/1 oz butter

115 g/4 oz caster sugar

1 tbsp elderflower cordial

300 ml/10 fl oz double cream

crisp biscuits, to serve

1 Top and tail the gooseberries and place in a saucepan with the butter. Over a gentle heat, slowly bring to the boil, stirring constantly, until the gooseberries are soft and turning yellow.

2 Remove from the heat and crush the berries with a wooden spoon until you have a thick purée. Add the sugar and stir until dissolved, then add the elderflower cordial. Taste for sweetness at this point and add a little more sugar if needed. Allow to cool.

3 Whip the cream until it is thick but not too dry. Using a metal spoon, fold in the cold gooseberry purée carefully. Only just combine the cream and the purée – the fool looks more attractive if it has a marbled effect.

4 Spoon into 6 glass serving dishes or 1 large glass bowl and chill well. Serve with crisp biscuits.

queen of puddings

SERVES 4–6

2 tbsp butter

600 ml/1 pint milk

115 g/4 oz fresh white breadcrumbs

115 g/4 oz caster sugar

grated rind of 1 lemon

3 eggs, separated

3 tbsp raspberry jam, warmed

1 tsp golden granulated sugar

1 Preheat the oven to 180°C/350°F/Gas Mark 4. Using a little of the butter, grease a 1-litre/1¾-pint baking dish.

2 Heat the remaining butter in the saucepan with the milk and gently bring to the boil over a medium heat. Remove from the heat and stir in the breadcrumbs, 1 tablespoon of the caster sugar and the lemon rind. Allow to stand and cool for 15 minutes, then beat in the egg yolks.

3 Pour the mixture into the baking dish, smooth the surface and bake in the centre of the oven for about 30 minutes until it is set. Spread over the jam.

4 Whisk the egg whites in a clean, grease-free mixing bowl until very thick, then gradually add the remaining caster sugar. Continue until all the sugar has been added.

5 Spoon the meringue over the pudding, making sure the meringue covers it completely. Swirl the meringue into attractive peaks and sprinkle with the granulated sugar.

6 Bake again in the centre of the oven for 10–15 minutes until the meringue is golden brown but still soft. Serve warm.

summer pudding

SERVES 6

675 g/1 lb 8 oz mixed soft fruits, such as redcurrants, blackcurrants, raspberries and blackberries

140 g/5 oz caster sugar

2 tbsp crème de framboise liqueur (optional)

6–8 slices of day-old white bread, crusts removed

double cream, to serve

1 Place the fruit in a large saucepan with the sugar. Over a low heat, very slowly bring to the boil, stirring carefully to ensure that the sugar has dissolved. Cook over a low heat for 2–3 minutes until the juices run but the fruit still holds its shape. Add the liqueur if using.

2 Line an 850-ml/1½-pint pudding basin with some of the slices of bread (cut them to shape so that the bread fits well). Spoon in the cooked fruit and juices, reserving a little of the juice for later.

3 Cover the surface of the fruit with the remaining bread. Place a saucer on top of the pudding and weight it down for at least 8 hours or overnight in the refrigerator.

4 Turn out the pudding onto a serving dish and pour over the reserved juices to colour any white bits of bread that may be showing. Serve immediately with the double cream.

lemon meringue pie

SERVES 6–8

pastry

150 g/5½ oz plain flour, plus extra for dusting

85 g/3 oz butter, cut into small pieces, plus extra for greasing

35 g/1¼ oz icing sugar, sifted

finely grated rind of ½ lemon

½ egg yolk, beaten

1½ tbsp milk

filling

3 tbsp cornflour

300 ml/10 fl oz water

juice and grated rind of 2 lemons

175 g/6 oz caster sugar

2 eggs, separated

1 To make the pastry, sift the flour into a bowl. Rub in the butter with your fingertips until the mixture resembles fine breadcrumbs. Mix in the remaining ingredients. Knead briefly on a lightly floured work surface. Wrap the pastry in clingfilm and allow it to rest for 30 minutes.

2 Preheat the oven to 180°C/350°F/Gas Mark 4. Grease a 20-cm/8-inch pie dish with butter. Roll out the pastry to a thickness of 5 mm/¼ inch; use it to line the base and sides of the dish. Prick all over with a fork, line with baking paper and fill with baking beans. Bake for 15 minutes. Remove the pastry case from the oven and take out the paper and beans. Reduce the temperature to 150°C/300°F/Gas Mark 2.

3 To make the filling, mix the cornflour with a little of the water. Put the remaining water in a saucepan. Stir in the lemon juice and rind and cornflour paste. Bring to the boil, stirring.

4 Cook for 2 minutes. Cool a little. Stir in 5 tablespoons of the sugar and the egg yolks and pour into the pastry case.

5 Whisk the egg whites in a clean, grease-free bowl until stiff. Gradually whisk in the remaining sugar. Spread the meringue over the pie. Bake for a further 40 minutes. Remove from oven, cool and serve.

sussex pond pudding

SERVES 6

225 g/8 oz self-raising flour

125 g/4½ oz vegetable suet

75 ml/5 tbsp milk

125 g/4½ oz unsalted butter, softened, plus extra for greasing

125 g/4½ oz soft light brown sugar

1 large unwaxed lemon

single cream, to serve

1 Lightly grease a 1.4-litre/2½-pint pudding basin. Mix the flour and suet together in a mixing bowl. Pour in the milk and mix to form a soft dough. Reserve one third of the dough to make a lid. Roll out the rest to a circle and press gently into the basin.

2 Cream the butter and sugar together and place on the dough in the basin. Prick the lemon all over and stand it, pointed end down, on top of the butter and sugar mixture. Roll the remaining pastry into a circle and lay it over the top of the basin, pressing the edges down well to seal.

3 Cover the basin with parchment paper and foil, making a pleat to allow the steam to rise. Tie with string around the rim. Fold some double thickness foil into a narrow strip to form a handle to lift the basin out of the pan.

4 Steam the pudding in a covered pan half-filled with water, for 3½–4 hours, topping up with boiling water when needed. Remove the foil and parchment and loosen the pudding with a knife. Turn the pudding onto a warmed serving plate and serve with cream.

sherry trifle

SERVES 8

100 g/3½ oz trifle sponges

150 ml/5 fl oz strawberry jam

250 ml/9 fl oz sherry

150 g/5½ oz fresh strawberries, hulled and sliced

400 g/14 oz canned mixed fruit, drained

1 large banana, sliced

for the custard layer

6 egg yolks

50 g/1¾ oz caster sugar

500 ml/18 fl oz milk

1 tsp vanilla extract

topping

300 ml/10 fl oz double cream

1–2 tbsp caster sugar

chocolate curls or flakes, to decorate

1 Spread the trifle sponges with jam, cut them into bite-sized cubes and arrange in the bottom of a large glass serving bowl. Pour over the sherry and leave for 30 minutes.

2 Combine the strawberries, canned fruit and banana and arrange over the sponges. Cover with clingfilm and chill for 30 minutes.

3 To make the custard, put the egg yolks and sugar into a bowl and whisk together. Pour the milk into a pan and warm gently over a low heat. Remove from the heat and gradually stir into the egg mixture, then return the mixture to the pan and stir constantly over a low heat until thickened. Do not boil. Remove from the heat, pour into a bowl and stir in the vanilla. Cool for 1 hour. Spread the custard over the trifle sponge and fruit mixture, cover with clingfilm and chill for 2 hours.

4 To make the topping, whip the cream in a bowl and stir in sugar to taste. Spread over the trifle, then scatter over the chocolate. Cover and refrigerate for at least 2 hours before serving.

treacle tart

SERVES 8

250 g/ 9 oz ready-made shortcrust pastry

plain flour, for dusting

350 g/12 oz golden syrup

125 g/4½ oz fresh white breadcrumbs

125 ml/4 fl oz double cream

finely grated rind of ½ lemon or orange

2 tbsp lemon juice or orange juice

whipped cream or clotted cream, to serve

1 Roll out the pastry on a lightly floured work surface and use to line a 20-cm/8-inch round loose-based tart tin, reserving the pastry trimmings. Prick the base of the pastry case all over with a fork, cover with clingfilm and chill in the refrigerator for 30 minutes. Re-roll the reserved pastry trimmings and cut out small shapes, such as hearts, leaves or stars, to decorate the top of the tart.

2 Preheat the oven to 190°C/375°F/Gas Mark 5. Mix the golden syrup, breadcrumbs, double cream and lemon rind with the lemon juice in a small bowl. Pour the mixture into the pastry case and decorate the top of the tart with the pastry shapes.

3 Transfer to the preheated oven and bake for 35–40 minutes, or until the filling is just set.

4 Leave the tart to cool slightly in the tin, then turn out and serve with cream.

eton mess

SERVES 4–6

3 egg whites

175 g/6 oz caster sugar

700 g/1 lb 9 oz strawberries, hulled

2 tbsp icing sugar

2 tbsp crème de fraise (strawberry) liqueur (optional)

300 ml/10 fl oz double cream

150 ml/5 fl oz single cream

1 Preheat the oven to 150°C/300°F/Gas Mark 2.

2 Whisk the egg whites in a mixing bowl until thick and forming soft peaks. Add the sugar gradually, whisking well after each addition. The meringue mixture should be glossy and firm.

3 Spoon the meringue onto a baking tray lined with baking paper and spread into a rough 30-cm/12-inch round. Cook in the preheated oven for 45–50 minutes until the meringue is firm on the outside but still soft in the centre. Remove from the oven and allow to cool.

4 Place a third of the strawberries (choose the larger ones) in a liquidizer and purée with the icing sugar. Pour the purée into a bowl, add the liqueur, if using, and the remaining strawberries and turn in the sauce until well mixed.

5 Whip together the double and single cream until thick but still light and floppy.

6 Break the meringue into large pieces and place half in a large glass serving bowl (or individual sundae dishes). Spoon over half the fruit mixture and half the cream. Layer up the remaining ingredients and lightly fold the mixture together so you have a streaky appearance. Serve immediately after mixing or the meringues will soften.

apple & blackberry crumble

SERVES 4

900 g/2 lb cooking apples

300 g/10½ oz blackberries, fresh or frozen

55 g/2 oz light muscovado sugar

1 tsp ground cinnamon

single or double cream, to serve

crumble topping

85 g/3 oz self-raising flour

85 g/3 oz plain wholemeal flour

115 g/4 oz unsalted butter

55 g/2 oz demerara sugar

1 Preheat the oven to 190°C/375°F/Gas Mark 5.

2 Peel and core the apples and cut into chunks. Place in a bowl with the blackberries, muscovado sugar and cinnamon and mix together, then transfer to an ovenproof baking dish.

3 To make the crumble topping, sift the self-raising flour into a bowl and stir in the wholemeal flour. Add the unsalted butter and rub in with your fingers until the mixture resembles fine breadcrumbs. Stir in the demerara sugar.

4 Spread the crumble over the apples and bake in the preheated oven for 40–45 minutes, or until the apples are soft and the crumble is golden brown and crisp.

5 Serve hot with cream.

VARIATION

Any seasonal fruit can be used in this crumble. Use rhubarb and increase the sugar to 115 g/4 oz and add the juice and rind of an orange. Or use equal quantities of apples and plums.

4

Time for Tea

toasted teacakes

MAKES 12

450 g/1 lb strong white flour, plus extra for dusting

1 sachet easy-blend dried yeast

50 g/1¾ oz caster sugar

1 tsp salt

2 tbsp butter, cut into small pieces, plus extra for greasing

300 ml/10 fl oz hand-hot milk

75 g/2¾ oz mixed dried fruit (sultanas, raisins, currants, mixed peel)

honey, for brushing

butter, to serve

1 Grease several baking trays with a little butter. Sift the flour into a large bowl. Stir in the yeast, sugar and salt. Add the butter and rub in with your fingertips until the mixture resembles fine breadcrumbs. Add the milk and mix together to form a soft dough.

2 Place the dough on a lightly floured work surface and knead for 5 minutes. Place the dough in a greased bowl, cover with clingfilm or a damp tea towel and leave to rise in a warm place for 1–1½ hours or until doubled in size.

3 Knead the dough again for a few minutes, then knead in the fruit. Divide the dough into 12 rounds and place on the baking trays. Cover and leave for 1 further hour, or until risen and springy to the touch.

4 Preheat the oven to 200°C/400°F/Gas Mark 6, then bake the teacakes for 20 minutes. Brush with honey while still warm, then transfer the teacakes to a wire rack to cool completely. Serve them split in half, toasted and spread with butter.

crumpets

MAKES 10–12

350 g/12 oz strong white flour

pinch of salt

1 sachet easy-blend dried yeast

1 tsp caster sugar

400 ml/14 fl oz tepid milk

butter, for greasing, plus extra to serve

1 Place the flour, salt, yeast and sugar in a bowl and mix well. Pour in the milk and mix everything together until the batter is smooth, beating the batter thoroughly so that it is light and airy. Cover with clingfilm and leave to rise in a warm place for 1 hour, or until well risen.

2 Stir the batter to knock out any air and check the consistency. If it is too thick, add 1 tablespoon of water (it should look rather gloopy). Set aside for 10 minutes.

3 Grease a large flat frying pan or griddle and 4 crumpet rings or 7.5-cm/3-inch plain metal cutters. Place the frying pan over a medium heat and leave to heat up for 2 minutes. Arrange the rings in the pan and spoon in enough batter to come halfway up each ring. Reduce the heat to low and cook for 5–6 minutes until small holes begin to appear and the top is starting to dry.

4 Remove the crumpet rings with a palette knife. Turn the crumpets over (the base should be golden brown) and cook the top for just 1–2 minutes to cook through. Keep the first batch of crumpets warm while you cook the rest of the batter.

5 Serve immediately with butter or, if you want to serve them later, allow them to cool and reheat in a toaster or under a grill.

hot cross buns

500 g/1 lb 2 oz strong white flour, plus extra for dusting

½ tsp salt

2 tsp ground mixed spice

1 tsp ground nutmeg

1 tsp ground cinnamon

2 tsp easy-blend dried yeast

50 g/1¾ oz golden caster sugar

finely grated rind of 1 lemon

175 g/6 oz currants

75 g/2¾ oz mixed peel

75 g/2¾ oz butter, melted

1 egg

225 ml/8 fl oz tepid milk

vegetable oil, for oiling

crosses

50 g/1¾ oz plain flour

25 g/1 oz butter, cut into pieces

1 tbsp cold water

glaze

3 tbsp milk

3 tbsp golden caster sugar

1 Sift the flour, salt and spices into a bowl and stir in the yeast, sugar, lemon rind, currants and mixed peel. Make a well in the centre. In a separate bowl, mix the melted butter, egg and milk. Pour into the dry ingredients and mix to make a soft dough, adding more milk if necessary. Brush a bowl with oil. Turn the dough out onto a floured work surface and knead for 10 minutes, or until smooth and elastic. Place the dough in the oiled bowl, cover with clingfilm and leave in a warm place for 1¾–2 hours, or until doubled in size.

2 Turn out onto a floured work surface, knead for 1–2 minutes, then divide into 12 balls. Place on a greased baking sheet, flatten slightly, then cover with oiled clingfilm. Leave in a warm place for 45 minutes, or until doubled in size. Preheat the oven to 220°C/425°F/Gas Mark 7.

3 To make the crosses, sift the flour into a bowl and rub in the butter. Stir in the cold water to make a dough. Divide into 24 strips, 18 cm/7 inches long. To make the glaze, place the milk and sugar in a saucepan over a low heat and stir until the sugar has dissolved. Brush some of the glaze over the buns and lay the pastry strips on them to form crosses. Bake in the preheated oven for 15–20 minutes, or until golden. Brush with the remaining glaze and return to the oven for 1 minute. Cool on a wire rack before serving.

scones & cream

MAKES 10–12

450 g/1 lb plain flour, plus extra for dusting

½ tsp salt

2 tsp baking powder

55 g/2 oz butter

2 tbsp caster sugar

250 ml/9 fl oz milk

3 tbsp milk, for glazing

strawberry jam and clotted cream, to serve

1 Preheat the oven to 220°C/425°F/Gas Mark 7.

2 Sift the flour, salt and baking powder into a bowl. Rub in the butter until the mixture resembles breadcrumbs. Stir in the sugar. Make a well in the centre and pour in the milk. Stir in using a round-bladed knife and make a soft dough.

3 Turn the mixture onto a floured surface and lightly flatten the dough until it is of an even thickness, about 1 cm/½ inch. Don't be heavy-handed, scones need a light touch.

4 Use a 6-cm/2½-inch pastry cutter to cut out the scones and place on the baking tray. Glaze with a little milk and bake in the preheated oven for 10–12 minutes, until golden and well risen.

5 Cool on a wire rack and serve freshly baked, with strawberry jam and clotted cream.

shortbread

MAKES 8 PIECES

175 g/6 oz plain flour, plus 1 tbsp for dusting

pinch of salt

55 g/2 oz caster sugar

115 g/4 oz butter, cut into small pieces, plus extra for greasing

2 tsp golden caster sugar

1 Grease a 20-cm/8-inch fluted cake tin or flan tin. Preheat the oven to 150°C/300°F/Gas Mark 2.

2 Mix together the flour, salt and caster sugar. Rub the butter into the dry ingredients. Continue to work the mixture until it forms a soft dough. Make sure you do not overwork the shortbread or it will be tough, not crumbly as it should be.

3 Lightly press the dough into the cake tin. If you don't have a fluted tin, roll out the dough on a lightly floured board, place on a baking tray and pinch the edges to form a scalloped pattern.

4 Mark into 8 pieces with a knife. Prick all over with a fork and bake in the centre of the oven for 45–50 minutes until the shortbread is firm and just coloured.

5 Allow to cool in the tin and dredge with the golden caster sugar. Cut into portions and remove to a wire rack. Store in an airtight container in a cool place until needed.

english muffins

MAKES 10–12

450 g/1 lb strong white flour, plus extra for dusting

½ tsp salt

1 tsp caster sugar

1½ tsp easy-blend dried yeast

250 ml/9 fl oz lukewarm water

125 ml/4 fl oz natural yogurt

vegetable oil, for oiling

40 g/1½ oz semolina

butter and jam, to serve

1 Sift the flour and salt together into a bowl and stir in the sugar and yeast. Make a well in the centre and add the water and yogurt. Stir with a wooden spoon until the dough begins to come together, then knead with your hands until it comes away from the side of the bowl. Turn out onto a lightly floured surface and knead for 5–10 minutes, until smooth and elastic.

2 Brush a bowl with oil. Shape the dough into a ball, put it in the bowl and cover with a damp tea towel. Leave to rise in a warm place for 30–40 minutes, until the dough has doubled in volume.

3 Dust a baking tray with flour. Turn out the dough onto a lightly floured surface and knead lightly. Roll out to a thickness of 2 cm/¾ inch. Stamp out 10–12 rounds with a 7.5-cm/3-inch biscuit cutter and sprinkle each round with semolina. Place on the baking tray, cover with a damp tea towel and leave to rise in a warm place for 30–40 minutes.

4 Heat a griddle or large frying pan over a medium–high heat and brush lightly with oil. Add half the muffins and cook for 7–8 minutes on each side, until golden brown. Cook the remaining muffins in the same way. Serve hot with butter and jam or cool, then split and toast them before serving.

fairy cupcakes

MAKES 16

115 g/4 oz unsalted butter

115 g/4 oz caster sugar

2 eggs, beaten

115 g/4 oz self-raising flour, sifted

sugar flowers, hundreds and thousands, glacé cherries, and/or chocolate strands, to decorate

icing

200 g/7 oz icing sugar

about 2 tbsp warm water

a few drops of food colouring (optional)

1 Preheat the oven to 190°C/375°F/Gas Mark 5. Put 16 paper baking cases in 2 bun trays or put 16 double-layer paper cases on a baking tray.

2 Place the butter and caster sugar in a large bowl and cream together with a wooden spoon or electric hand whisk until pale and fluffy.

3 Gradually add the eggs, beating well after each addition. Fold in the flour lightly and evenly using a metal spoon. Spoon the mixture into the paper cases and bake in the preheated oven for 15–20 minutes. Cool on a wire rack.

4 For the icing, sift the icing sugar into a bowl and stir in just enough water to mix to a smooth paste that is thick enough to coat the back of a wooden spoon. Stir in a few drops of food colouring, if using, then spread the icing over the fairy cakes and decorate as desired.

brandy snaps

MAKES 20

85 g/3 oz unsalted butter

**85 g/3 oz golden caster
sugar**

3 tbsp golden syrup

85 g/3 oz plain flour

1 tsp ground ginger

1 tbsp brandy

**finely grated rind
of ½ lemon**

filling

**150 ml/5 fl oz double
cream or whipping
cream**

1 tbsp brandy (optional)

1 tbsp icing sugar

1 Preheat the oven to 160°C/325°F/Gas Mark 3. Line three large baking trays with baking paper.

2 Place the butter, sugar and golden syrup in a saucepan and heat gently over a low heat, stirring occasionally, until melted. Remove from the heat and leave to cool slightly. Sift the flour and ginger into the pan and beat until smooth, then stir in the brandy and lemon rind. Drop small spoonfuls of the mixture onto the prepared baking trays, leaving plenty of room for spreading. Place one baking tray at a time in the preheated oven for 10–12 minutes, or until the snaps are golden brown.

3 Remove the first baking tray from the oven and cool for about 30 seconds, then lift each snap with a palette knife and wrap around the handle of a wooden spoon. If they start to become too firm to wrap, return them to the oven for about 30 seconds to soften. When firm, remove from the spoon handles and cool on a wire rack. Repeat with the remaining baking trays.

4 For the filling, whip the cream with the brandy, if using, and icing sugar until thick. Just before serving, pipe the cream mixture into each end of the brandy snaps.

rich fruit cake

SERVES 16

350 g/12 oz sultanas

225 g/8 oz raisins

115 g/4 oz ready-to-eat dried apricots, chopped

85 g/3 oz stoned dates, chopped

4 tbsp dark rum or brandy, plus extra for flavouring (optional)

finely grated rind and juice of 1 orange

oil or melted butter, for greasing

225 g/8 oz unsalted butter

225 g/8 oz light muscovado sugar

4 eggs

70 g/2½ oz chopped mixed peel

85 g/3 oz glacé cherries, quartered

25 g/1 oz chopped glacé ginger or stem ginger

40 g/1½ oz blanched almonds, chopped

200 g/7 oz plain flour

1 tsp ground mixed spice

1 Place the sultanas, raisins, apricots and dates in a large bowl and stir in the rum, orange rind and orange juice. Cover and leave to soak for several hours or overnight.

2 Preheat the oven to 150°C/300°F/Gas Mark 2. Grease a 20-cm/8-inch round deep cake tin and line the base with baking paper.

3 Cream together the butter and sugar until light and fluffy. Gradually beat in the eggs, beating hard after each addition. Stir in the soaked fruits, mixed peel, glacé cherries, glacé ginger and blanched almonds.

4 Sift together the flour and mixed spice, then fold lightly and evenly into the mixture. Spoon the mixture into the prepared cake tin and level the surface, making a slight depression in the centre with the back of the spoon.

5 Bake in the preheated oven for 2¼–2¾ hours, or until the cake is beginning to shrink away from the sides and a skewer inserted into the centre comes out clean. Cool completely in the tin.

6 Turn out the cake and remove the lining paper. Wrap in greaseproof paper and foil, and store for at least two months before use. To add a richer flavour, prick the cake with a skewer and spoon over a couple of extra tablespoons of rum or brandy, if using, before storing.

victoria sponge cake

SERVES 8–10

175 g/6 oz butter, at room temperature, plus extra for greasing

175 g/6 oz caster sugar

3 eggs, beaten

175 g/6 oz self-raising flour

pinch of salt

3 tbsp raspberry jam

1 tbsp caster or icing sugar

1 Preheat the oven to 180°C/350°F/Gas Mark 4. Grease two 20-cm/8-inch sponge tins and line with greaseproof paper or baking paper.

2 Cream the butter and sugar together until light and fluffy. Add the egg a little at a time, beating well after each addition.

3 Sift the flour and salt and carefully add to the mixture, folding it in with a metal spoon or a spatula. Divide the mixture between the tins and smooth over with the spatula.

4 Place them on the same shelf in the centre of the oven and bake for 25–30 minutes until well risen, golden brown and beginning to shrink from the sides of the tin. Remove from the oven and allow to stand for 1 minute.

5 Loosen the cakes from around the edge of the tins using a palette knife. Turn the cakes out onto a clean tea towel, remove the paper and invert them onto a wire rack (this prevents the wire rack from marking the top of the cakes).

6 When completely cool, sandwich together with the jam and sprinkle with the sugar. The cake is delicious when freshly baked, but any remaining cake can be stored in an airtight tin for up to 1 week.

madeira cake

SERVES 8–10

**175 g/6 oz unsalted butter,
plus extra for greasing**

175 g/6 oz caster sugar

**finely grated rind of 1
lemon**

3 large eggs, beaten

115 g/4 oz plain flour

115 g/4 oz self-raising flour

2–3 tbsp brandy or milk

2 slices of citron peel

1 Preheat the oven to 160°C/325°F/Gas Mark 3. Grease and line an 18-cm/7-inch round deep cake tin.

2 Cream together the butter and sugar until pale and fluffy. Add the lemon rind and gradually beat in the eggs. Sift in the flours and fold in evenly, adding enough brandy to make a soft dropping consistency.

3 Spoon the mixture into the prepared tin and smooth the surface. Lay the slices of citron peel on top of the cake.

4 Bake in the preheated oven for 1–1¼ hours, or until well risen, golden brown and springy to the touch.

5 Cool in the tin for 10 minutes, then turn out and cool completely on a wire rack.

parkin

SERVES 10–12

butter, for greasing

150 g/5½ oz self-raising flour

pinch of salt

½ tsp mixed spice

2 tsp ground ginger

200 g/7 oz medium oatmeal

175 g/6 oz black treacle

100 g/3½ oz butter

85 g/3 oz soft brown sugar

1 tbsp milk

1 egg, beaten

1 Preheat the oven to 140°C/275°F/Gas Mark 1. Lightly grease a 15cm-/6-inch square cake tin and line the base with baking parchment.

2 Sift the flour into a mixing bowl and stir in the salt, spices and oatmeal. Make a well in the centre.

3 Place the treacle, butter and sugar into a pan and melt slowly over a medium heat, without allowing the mixture to boil. Pour the melted mixture into the well of the dry ingredients and gently combine. Stir in the milk and egg and mix until smooth.

4 Pour the mixture into the prepared tin and bake in the preheated oven for 1¾–2 hours, or until a skewer inserted in the centre comes out clean.

5 Leave to cool in the tin for 30 minutes, then turn out on a wire rack to cool completely. Store in an airtight container in a cool place for at least a week before cutting, to allow it to become moist and sticky.

chocolate fudge cake

175 g/6 oz unsalted butter, softened, plus extra for greasing

175 g/6 oz golden caster sugar

3 eggs, beaten

3 tbsp golden syrup

40 g/1½ oz ground almonds

175 g/6 oz self-raising flour

pinch of salt

40 g/1½ oz cocoa powder

icing

225 g/8 oz plain chocolate, broken into pieces

55 g/2 oz dark muscovado sugar

225 g/8 oz unsalted butter, diced

5 tbsp evaporated milk

½ tsp vanilla extract

1 Preheat the oven to 180°C/350°F/Gas Mark 4. Grease and line the bases of two 20-cm/8-inch sandwich tins.

2 To make the icing, place the chocolate, muscovado sugar, butter, evaporated milk and vanilla extract in a heavy-based saucepan. Heat gently, stirring constantly, until melted. Pour into a bowl and leave to cool. Cover and chill in the refrigerator for 1 hour, or until spreadable.

3 For the cake, place the butter and caster sugar in a bowl and beat together until light and fluffy. Gradually beat in the eggs. Stir in the golden syrup and ground almonds. Sift the flour, salt and cocoa powder into a separate bowl, then fold into the mixture. Add a little water, if necessary, to make a dropping consistency.

4 Spoon the mixture into the prepared tins and bake in the preheated oven for 30–35 minutes, or until springy to the touch and a skewer inserted in the centre comes out clean.

5 Leave the cakes in the tins for 5 minutes, then turn out onto wire racks to cool completely. When the cakes are cold, sandwich them together with half the icing. Spread the remaining icing over the top and sides of the cake, swirling it to give a frosted appearance.

lemon drizzle cake

SERVES 8

**oil or melted butter,
for greasing**

200 g/7 oz plain flour

2 tsp baking powder

200 g/7 oz caster sugar

4 eggs

**150 ml/5 fl oz soured
cream**

**grated rind of 1 large
lemon**

4 tbsp lemon juice

150 ml/5 fl oz sunflower oil

syrup

4 tbsp icing sugar

3 tbsp lemon juice

1 Preheat the oven to 180°C/350°F/Gas Mark 4. Lightly grease a 20-cm/8-inch loose-based round cake tin and line the base with baking paper.

2 Sift the flour and baking powder into a mixing bowl and stir in the caster sugar. In a separate bowl, whisk the eggs, soured cream, lemon rind, lemon juice and oil together. Pour the egg mixture into the dry ingredients and mix well until evenly combined.

3 Pour the mixture into the prepared tin and bake in the preheated oven for 45–60 minutes, until risen and golden brown.

4 For the syrup, mix together the icing sugar and lemon juice in a small saucepan. Stir over a low heat until just beginning to bubble and turn syrupy.

5 As soon as the cake comes out of the oven, prick the surface with a fine skewer, then brush the syrup over the top. Leave the cake to cool completely in the tin before turning out and serving.

date & walnut loaf

SERVES 8

100 g/3½ oz stoned dates, chopped

½ tsp bicarbonate of soda

finely grated rind of ½ lemon

100 ml/3½ fl oz hot tea

40 g/1½ oz unsalted butter, plus extra for greasing

70 g/2½ oz light muscovado sugar

1 small egg

125 g/4½ oz self-raising flour

25 g/1 oz walnuts, chopped

walnut halves, to decorate

1 Preheat the oven to 180°C/350°F/Gas Mark 4. Grease a 450-g/1-lb loaf tin and line the base with baking paper. Place the dates, bicarbonate of soda and lemon rind in a bowl and add the hot tea. Leave to soak for 10 minutes, until soft.

2 Cream together the butter and sugar until light and fluffy, then beat in the egg. Stir in the date mixture.

3 Fold in the flour using a large metal spoon, then fold in the walnuts. Spoon the mixture into the prepared cake tin and spread evenly. Top with walnut halves.

4 Bake in the preheated oven for 35–40 minutes, or until risen, firm and golden brown. Cool for 10 minutes in the tin, then turn out the loaf and finish cooling on a wire rack.

chelsea buns

MAKES 9

225 g/8 oz strong white flour, plus extra for dusting

½ tsp salt

1½ tsp easy-blend dried yeast

1 tsp golden caster sugar

2 tbsp butter, diced, plus extra for greasing

125 ml/4 fl oz tepid milk

1 egg, beaten

85 g/3 oz icing sugar

filling

55 g/2 oz light muscovado sugar

115 g/4 oz luxury mixed dried fruit

1 tsp ground mixed spice

4 tbsp butter, softened

1 Grease an 18-cm/7-inch square cake tin. Sift the flour and salt together, then stir in the yeast and caster sugar. Rub in the butter until the mixture resembles breadcrumbs. Mix the milk and egg together and mix into the flour to form a soft dough. Turn out the dough on a lightly floured work surface and knead for 5–10 minutes, or until smooth and elastic. Put in an oiled bowl, cover with clingfilm or a damp tea towel and leave to rise in a warm place for 1 hour, or until doubled in size.

2 Turn out the dough again and knead lightly for 1 minute. Roll out into a rectangle 30 x 23 cm/12 x 9 inches. Mix the muscovado sugar, dried fruit and mixed spice together in a bowl. Spread the dough with the butter and sprinkle the fruit mixture on top. Roll up, starting from one long edge. Cut into 9 slices and arrange in the tin. Cover and leave to rise in a warm place for 45 minutes. Preheat the oven to 190°C/375°F/Gas Mark 5.

3 Bake the buns for 30 minutes, or until golden. Cool in the tin for 10 minutes, then transfer, in one piece, to a wire rack to cool completely. Mix the icing sugar with just enough water to make a thin glaze. Brush over the buns and leave to set. Pull the buns apart to serve.

home-made oat crackers with british cheeses

MAKES ABOUT
30 CRACKERS

115 g/4 oz wholemeal flour,
plus extra for rolling

1 tsp baking powder

½ tsp salt

140 g/5 oz fine oatmeal

85 g/3 oz butter,
plus extra for greasing

1 tbsp caster sugar

4 tbsp cold water

to serve

British cheeses, such as
Cheddar, Somerset Brie,
Stilton and Cornish Yarg

grapes and figs

1 Preheat the oven to 180°C/350°F/Gas Mark 4 and lightly grease 2 baking sheets.

2 Sieve the flour, baking powder and salt into a mixing bowl, then mix in the oatmeal. Add the butter and rub it into the dry ingredients. Spoon in the sugar and the water and mix to a smooth dough. Turn the mixture onto a floured surface and knead until smooth.

3 Roll the dough out until 3 mm/⅛ inch thick, then cut out the crackers using a 6-cm/2½-inch round cutter.

4 Place the biscuits onto the prepared baking sheets and bake for about 15 minutes until golden. Change the position of the sheets in the oven halfway through the cooking time to ensure even cooking. Remove from the oven and lift the biscuits onto a wire rack to cool.

5 Serve the oat crackers with a variety of British cheeses and some grapes and figs.

barm brack

MAKES 1 LOAF

**650 g/1 lb 7 oz strong white
flour, plus extra for
dusting**

1 tsp mixed spice

1 tsp salt

**2 tsp easy-blend
dried yeast**

1 tbsp golden caster sugar

**300 ml/10 fl oz
lukewarm milk**

**150 ml/5 fl oz
lukewarm water**

vegetable oil, for oiling

**4 tbsp softened butter, plus
extra to serve**

**325 g/11½ oz mixed
dried fruit (sultanas,
currants and raisins)**

milk, for glazing

1 Sift the flour, mixed spice and salt into a warmed bowl.
Stir in the yeast and caster sugar. Make a well in the centre
and pour in the milk and water. Mix together to make a sticky
dough. Turn the dough out onto a lightly floured work surface
and knead until no longer sticky. Put the dough in an oiled bowl,
cover with clingfilm and leave to rise in a warm place for 1 hour,
until doubled in size.

2 Turn the dough out onto a floured work surface and knead
lightly for 1 minute. Add the butter and dried fruit to the
dough and work them in until completely incorporated. Return
the dough to the bowl, replace the clingfilm and leave to rise
for 30 minutes.

3 Oil a 23-cm/9-inch round cake tin. Pat the dough to a neat
round and fit in the tin. Cover and leave in a warm place
until it has risen to the top of the tin. Meanwhile, preheat
the oven to 200°C/400°F/Gas Mark 6.

4 Brush the top of the loaf lightly with milk and bake in the
preheated oven for 15 minutes. Cover the loaf with foil,
reduce the oven temperature to 180°C/350°F/Gas Mark 4 and
bake for a further 45 minutes, until golden brown and it sounds
hollow when tapped on the bottom. Transfer to a wire rack and
leave to cool. Serve sliced, with butter.

crusty white bread

MAKES 1 LOAF

1 egg

1 egg yolk

150–200 ml/5–7 fl oz lukewarm water

500 g/1 lb 2 oz strong white flour, plus extra for dusting

1½ tsp salt

2 tsp sugar

1 tsp easy-blend dried yeast

25 g/1 oz butter, diced

sunflower oil, for greasing

1 Place the egg and egg yolk in a jug and beat lightly to mix. Add enough lukewarm water to make up to 300 ml/10 fl oz. Stir well.

2 Place the flour, salt, sugar and yeast in a large bowl. Add the butter and rub it in with your fingertips until the mixture resembles breadcrumbs. Make a well in the centre, add the egg mixture and work to a smooth dough.

3 Turn out onto a lightly floured surface and knead well for about 10 minutes, until smooth. Brush a bowl with oil. Shape the dough into a ball, place it in the bowl and cover with a damp tea towel. Leave to rise in a warm place for 1 hour, until the dough has doubled in size.

4 Oil a 900-g/2-lb loaf tin. Turn out the dough onto a lightly floured surface and knead for 1 minute until smooth. Shape the dough to the length of the tin and three times the width. Fold the dough into three lengthways and place it in the tin with the join underneath. Cover and leave in a warm place for 30 minutes, until it has risen above the tin. Preheat the oven to 220°C/425°F/Gas Mark 7.

5 Place the dough in the preheated oven and bake for 30 minutes, or until firm and golden brown. Test that the loaf is cooked by tapping on the base with your knuckles – it should sound hollow. Transfer to a wire rack to cool.

granary bread

MAKES 1 LOAF

500 g/1lb 2 oz granary bread flour, plus extra for dusting

1 tbsp olive oil, plus extra for oiling

1½ tsp salt

1½ tsp easy-blend dried yeast

1 tbsp clear honey

275 ml/9 fl oz warm water

1 Place the flour, oil, salt and yeast in a large bowl and mix together. Add the honey to the water, pour into the dry ingredients, and mix together to form a soft dough. If it is very sticky add a little more flour.

2 Turn the dough out onto on a lightly floured or oiled worktop, and knead for 10 minutes.

3 Place the dough back in the mixing bowl and cover with lightly oiled clingfilm. Leave in a warm place for about 1½ hours, or until doubled in size.

4 Turn the dough out and knead again gently for one minute. Grease a 900-g/2-lb loaf tin. Put the dough in the tin, cover and leave in a warm place to rise again for about 30 minutes.

5 Preheat the oven to 200°C/400°F/Gas Mark 6. Bake the loaf for 35–40 minutes until golden and risen and the bottom sounds hollow when tapped. Transfer to a wire rack to cool.

irish soda bread

MAKES 1 LOAF

butter, for greasing

450 g/1 lb plain flour, plus extra for dusting

1 tsp salt

1 tsp bicarbonate of soda

400 ml/14 fl oz buttermilk

1 Preheat the oven to 220°C/425°F/Gas Mark 7. Lightly grease a baking tray.

2 Sift the flour, salt and bicarbonate of soda into a mixing bowl. Make a well in the centre of the dry ingredients and pour in most of the buttermilk.

3 Mix well together using your hands. The dough should be very soft but not too wet. If necessary, add the remaining buttermilk.

4 Turn out the dough onto a lightly floured surface and knead it lightly. Shape into a 20-cm/8-inch round.

5 Place the bread on the prepared baking tray, cut a cross in the top and bake in the preheated oven for 25–30 minutes. Test that the loaf is cooked by tapping on the base with your knuckles – it should sound hollow. Transfer onto a wire rack to cool slightly. Serve warm.

cottage loaf

MAKES 1 LOAF

**675 g/1 lb 8 oz strong white
flour, plus extra for
dusting**

2 tsp salt

**1 sachet easy-blend dried
yeast**

**400 ml/14 fl oz lukewarm
water**

vegetable oil, for brushing

1 Place the flour, salt and yeast in a large bowl. Make a well in the centre, pour in the water and work to a smooth dough. Turn out onto a lightly floured surface and knead well for about 10 minutes, until smooth. Shape the dough into a ball, place it in an oiled bowl and cover with a damp tea towel. Leave to rise in a warm place for 1 hour, or until the dough has doubled in size.

2 Brush 2 baking sheets with oil. Turn out the dough onto a lightly floured surface and knead for 1 minute until smooth. Shape the dough into two balls, one about twice the size of the other. Put them on the baking sheets, cover and leave to rise in a warm place for 30 minutes.

3 With a floured hand, gently flatten the larger ball of dough. Cut a 5-cm/2-inch cross in the centre of the top and brush with water. Put the smaller ball of dough on top. Make small vertical slashes all around both pieces of dough. Brush the handle of a wooden spoon with the oil and push it into the centre of the loaf to make a hole through both pieces of dough. Put the loaf on the baking sheet, cover and leave in a warm place for 15 minutes.

4 Preheat the oven to 220°C/425°F/Gas Mark 7. Bake the loaf for 40 minutes, until the crust is golden brown and it sounds hollow when tapped on the base with your knuckles. Transfer to a wire rack to cool.

strawberry jam

MAKES ABOUT
1.5 KG/ 3 LB 5 OZ

1.5 kg/3 lb 5 oz ripe,
unblemished whole
strawberries, hulled
and rinsed

2 freshly squeezed lemons,
juice sieved

1.5 kg/3 lb 5 oz jam sugar

1 tsp butter

1 Place the strawberries in a preserving pan with the lemon juice, then simmer over a gentle heat for 15–20 minutes, stirring occasionally, until the fruit has collapsed and is very soft.

2 Add the sugar and heat, stirring occasionally, until the sugar has completely dissolved. Add the butter, then bring to the boil and boil rapidly for 10–20 minutes, or until the setting point is reached.

3 Test the mixture with a sugar thermometer – it should read 105°C/221°F for a good setting point. Alternatively, drop a teaspoonful of the mixture onto a cold saucer, place it in the refrigerator to cool, and then push it with your finger. If it forms a wrinkled skin, it is ready. If not, boil for a further minute and repeat.

4 Leave to cool for 8–10 minutes, skim off any foam then pot into warmed sterilized jars and cover the tops with waxed discs. When completely cold, cover with cellophane or lids, label and store in a cool place.

lemon curd

MAKES 700 G/1 LB 9 OZ

3 unwaxed lemons

350 g/12 oz caster sugar

3 eggs, beaten

**175 g/6 oz butter, cut into
small pieces**

1 Carefully grate the rind from each of the lemons using a
fine grater. Make sure you take only the yellow rind and
not the bitter white pith.

2 Halve the lemons, squeeze out all the juice and strain to
remove the pips.

3 Place a medium-sized heatproof bowl over a saucepan of
simmering water and add the lemon rind, juice and sugar.
Mix together well until the sugar has dissolved.

4 Add the eggs and the butter and continue to stir for
25–30 minutes until the butter has melted and the
mixture begins to thicken. Beat well and turn into sterilized
jars. Cover and label before storing. Once opened, the lemon
curd will keep for up to 2 months in the refrigerator.

VARIATION

Most citrus fruit can be used to make curd – instead of lemons
use the zest and juice of other citrus fruit, making sure that it
makes 150ml. For example, use the juice of 2 large oranges, plus
half a lemon, or 4 limes for a tangy alternative.